JULIO-CLAUDIAN BUILDING PROGRAMS:

A Quantitative Study in Political Management

M.K. and R.L. THORNTON

JULIO-CLAUDIAN BUILDING PROGRAMS:
A Quantitative Study in Political Management

M.K. and R.L. Thornton

Bolchazy-Carducci Publishers

Paperback Cover: Front View of the Maison Carrée
It is a typical Roman temple with its high podium and is the
best externally preserved temple of the Augustan age. It
provides the base number from which the work unit system
is calculated. (Photo courtesy of Robert M. Wilhelm)

DGL9
T48
1989

©Copyright 1989

BOLCHAZY-CARDUCCI PUBLISHERS
1000 Brown Street, Unit 101
Wauconda, IL 60084

Printed in the United States of America

International Standard Book Number:
Hardbound   0-86516-203-4
Softbound   0-86516-202-6

Library of Congress Catalog Card Number:
88-62696

Library of Congress Cataloging-in-Publication Data

Thornton, M. K., 1920–
    Julio-Claudian building programs : a quantitative study in
political management / M. K. and R. L. Thornton.
        p.   cm.
    Bibliography: p.
    Includes index.
    ISBN 0-86516-203-4 : $35.00. — ISBN 0-86516-202-6 (pbk.) : $20.00
    1. Rome (Italy)—Public works—Management—History.   2. Food
supply—Government policy—Italy—Rome—History.   3. Manpower
policy—Italy—Rome—History.   4. Rome (Italy)—Politics and
government.   I. Thornton, R. L., 1917–   .   II. Title.
DG69.T48   1989
320.937—dc20   88-62696
                                                         CIP

ACKNOWLEDGEMENTS

We are indebted to Professor M.T. Boatwright for reading an earlier version of this book, for suggesting helpful changes in its organization and for voicing challenging contrary opinions on selected issues. We, of course, retain full responsibility for the contents of the book.

We express our gratitude also to Dr. Joseph Plescia for his helpful suggestions at various points in the manuscript. We thank Miami University for a grant that was an aid in the preparation of this book; we thank its Audio-Visual Center for its graphic work.

ABBREVIATIONS

AHR	*American Historical Review*
AJA	*American Journal of Archaeology*
AJP	*American Journal of Philology*
AncW	*The Ancient World*
ANRW	*Aufstieg und Niedergang der römischen Welt* ed. H. Temporini (Berlin & New York, 1972–)
BMC Emp.	*Coins of the Roman Empire in the British Museum*, vol. I, ed. H. Mattingly (1923)
Brisse	A. Brisse, *The Draining of Lake Fucino* trans. by V. de Tivoli (Rome, 1876)
CIL	*Corpus Inscriptionum Latinarum*
CP	*Classical Philology*
ESAR	*Economic Survey of Ancient Rome* ed. T. Frank (Baltimore, 1940), V.
IJNA	*International Journal of Nautical Archaeology*
JFA	*Journal of Field Archaeology*
JRS	*Journal of Roman Studies*
Meiggs	R. Meiggs, *Roman Ostia* (Oxford, 1973), 2nd edition
Nash	E. Nash, *Pictorial Dictionary of Ancient Rome,* 2 vols. (New York, 1968, 2nd edition)
Platner-Ashby	S. Platner and T. Ashby, *A Topographical Dictionary of Ancient Rome* (London, 1929)
RE	*Real-Encyclopädie der Klassischen Altertumswissenschaft*
RG	*Res Gestae Divi Augusti*
Rodewald	C. Rodewald, *Money in the Age of Tiberius* (Manchester, 1976)
Strong	D.E. Strong, "Administration of Public Building in Rome During The Late Republic and Early Empire," *Bulletin of Institute of Classical Studies* 15 (1968), 97–109
TAPA	*Transactions and Proceedings of the American Philological Association*

PREFACE

Rome's Julio-Claudian period represents an era of remarkable growth, of administrative innovation, and of economic affluence. It represents a turning point so great as to leave an indelible imprint on Western civilization, so great as to rival in importance the industrial revolution, so great as to create one of history's longest recorded periods of peace and of prosperity.

In this study we hope to provide an understanding of the intertwining of the political and economic forces during the Julio-Claudian period; we will use as a unifying force the imperial public works programs with their political roots in the needs of the society and with their economic impact shown through their manpower demands.

The period of change might have started earlier; indeed, Julius Caesar was the first ruler to see the evolving demands of the Empire. He was the first to see that Rome's role had changed and to plan for measures appropriate for her imperial destiny. Caesar had envisioned many of the projects important to the Julio-Claudians. For example, he did forward planning for measures to insure the food supply of an imperial capital which could no longer feed herself (Plut. *Caes.* 58. 10). Caesar's murder, however, demonstrated that political changes were necessary: the Roman Revolution needed to be completed. Rome had to develop new political systems with a centralized power, consisting of a deliberative branch (the Senate) and a powerful executive branch (the Emperor), capable of making positive decisions to carry them out. In the words of Ronald Syme: "It was the end of a century of anarchy, culminating in twenty years of civil war and military tyranny. If despotism was the price, it was not too high."[1] By 27 B.C. the despot had been found.

ORGANIZATION OF THE BOOK

In the subsequent chapters we will discuss the following topics:

1. The environment in which the public works program took place; the sources for our information, and the assumptions we found necessary to make.

2. A project by project evaluation of the manpower cost associated with the public building program, organized by year and by reign.
3. The institutions and industrial organization through which public works were carried out; does it matter whether the labor force consists of freedmen or of slaves?
4. Earlier Julio-Claudians: A preliminary evaluation of the realities of the study and of the cyclical patterns which appeared because of the varying objectives and policies of the emperors.
5. An in-depth study of an outlier project, that of the draining of the Fucine Lake, first as a data check-point and secondly as an explanation of certain of the cyclical patterns of work.
6. An evaluation of a second outlier project, that of the building of the Harbor of Ostia, to fit its demands into the political and industrial pattern of the rulers involved.
7. The later Julio-Claudians.
8. Conclusions and implications.

The core of the study is the project by project evaluation contained in Chapter 2. Based on the patterns thus discerned, we will then focus on the performance of the emperors in managing their building programs. Finally, we will evaluate the leaders philosophically as to whether they performed, as Syme suggests, from the inevitability of events or whether the rulers decided from individual creativity. In other words, was the history made by the men or by the march of time? We will test Syme's statement that "the conviction that it all had to happen is indeed difficult to discard."[2]

SOME NOTES TO OUR READERS

First, we think the core of our readers will be academics who specialize in Classics or in Roman History. An important group of the historians will be Economic historians, whose academic home will be among the economists rather than among the historians. We hope a few of you will be political scientists. Because of the innovations we have attempted in measuring techniques and the technical problems we have tried to control, some interest should come from students of the history of technology, some of whom reside in Engineering Schools. Lastly, and important for us even to the extent of some softening of the rigor of the academic vernacular are the informed amateurs. We have already met some of these through questions posed on a portion of this book, previously published as an article on the draining of the Fucine Lake. So diverse an assortment of readers has given us problems in meeting the needs of one group without irritating a separate group with different backgrounds. We apologize to both sides of such controversies for the problems which come from compromise. We have, however, tried always to live up to the academic rigor required in our treatment of available information.

We have made some concessions to meet the different needs of our readers: First, our underlying data and our presentation of detailed calculations are essential to academic credibility. However, the arithmetic involved is complicated enough to interfere with the smooth flow of the ideas presented. An academic wants his facts along with his conclusions. Other readers may not wish to follow the detailed stream of calculations. Our compromise is to put the arithmetic details in the appendices. We hope our rigorous friends will be willing to search. Had we done the reverse, our less rigorous friends would have lost interest. There is a more detailed level of information at the most basic end of our data gathering. This consists of a project by project measurement of dimensions, of analysis of materials used, of the degree to which certain work was original building and which was renovation. In much of this we made judgments on various specific details. The sum of this is a mass of details most of which does not have an impact on our conclusions but which is subject to technical modernization as new data become available. The 5 × 8 cards on which we did our calculations are stored in the University Archives of Miami University in Oxford, Ohio, 45056 and can be made available on request to scholars. Since our technique of comparative work measurements is innovative, we are particularly interested in comments which might standardize and improve the technique or offer different alternate techniques to meet the same need.

Some of our readers may be surprised at the inclusion of our detailed discussion of "factotums" in the chapter on conclusions. We have done this intentionally. The concept of "factotums" was not in our plans. It arose forcefully as we studied the differences in management techniques of different emperors. It thus sprang up as a conclusion. In understanding the concept the reader must see it surfacing as the treatment of different emperors occurs. It is not of value until the whole set has been studied. We believe that treatment as a conclusion is thus appropriate.

We have one other "mea culpa". We have used the label "Julio-Claudian" to cover Augustus as well as his appropriate successors. Rigorous scholars will object. We have two reasons for wanting to include Augustus. First, he really laid down the building policies that affected the later emperors so a discussion of his policies is a necessary background for understanding the subsequent policies of the Julio-Claudians. Second, to us the changeover to Tiberius from Augustus is a smooth flow, not a specific event. The decision making authority on building programs started to change with the death of Agrippa in 12 B.C. At that time Tiberius inherited the task, one which carried his clear imprint from then to his own death in A.D. 37. We use the term Julio-Claudian to cover the period from 27 B.C. to A.D. 68. We hope that you will readjust your understandings if you must.

ENDNOTES TO PREFACE

¹*The Roman Revolution* (London, 1939), 2.
²*Rom. Rev.*, 4.

CONTENTS

Acknowledgements   v

Abbreviations   vii

Preface   ix

List of Illustrations   xiv

   I.   Introduction   3

   II.   Manpower Costs of the Building Programs   15

   III.   Administration of Public Works and
              Labor Management   31

   IV.   Earlier Julio-Claudian Emperors   41

   V.   The Draining of the Fucine Lake   57

   VI.   The Harbor of Ostia   77

   VII.   The Later Julio-Claudian Emperors   93

   VIII.   Implications and Conclusions   103

Bibliography   125

Appendices   1. Method of Determining the WUs for
                    Certain Other Constructions   131

               2. List of All Julio-Claudian
                    Building Projects   135

               3. Fucine Lake   141

               4. Harbor of Ostia   145

Index   151

LIST OF ILLUSTRATIONS

1. Front View of Maison Carrée
   Courtesy: Robert M. Wilhelm   cover

2. Map: The Roman Empire at the Time of Augustus
   A.D. 14.
   Courtesy: Macmillan Publishing Co.*   xvi–xvii

3. Reconstruction of Thermae of Agrippa
   (from Hülsen, 1910)
   Courtesy: Fototeca Unione 2963†   8

4. Thermae of Agrippa in the via della Ciambella
   Courtesy: Fototeca Unione 4261   9

5. Rome in the Time of the Emperors
   Courtesy: Macmillan Publishing Co.*   16

6. Maison Carrée (Nîmes, France)
   Courtesy: Fototeca Unione 11202   17

7. Chart 1. Total Work Units. Julio-Claudian Emperors
   Source: M. K. and R. L. Thornton   28

8. Data Sheet for Chart 1
   Source: M. K. and R. L. Thornton   29

9. Aqua Claudia and Anio Novus on Porta Praenestina
   Courtesy: Fototeca Unione 848   30

10. Theater of Marcellus
    Courtesy: Fototeca Unione 536   42

11. Mausoleum of Augustus
    Courtesy: Fototeca Unione 1076   45

12. Aqua Claudia coming into Rome
    Courtesy: Fototeca Unione 845   52

13. Porta Praenestina, Rome
    Courtesy: Fototeca Unione 5651   54

14. Map: Italy and Fucine Lake   56

15. Chart. Variations in Depth of Lake Fucine
     Source: M. K. and R. L. Thornton   58

16. Mount Salviano
     Source: after Brisse, Miami University
     Audio-Visual   60

17. Corinthian painted *pinax*
     Courtesy: Staatliche Museen zu Berlin   62

18. Ports of Claudius and Trajan
     Courtesy: Fototeca Unione 11055   78

19. Chart 2. Harbor of Ostia
     Source: M. K. and R. L. Thornton   82

20. Sestertius of Nero
     Courtesy: British Museum, London   86

21. Map: Ostia
     Courtesy: Macmillan Publishing Co.*   91

22. The Claudian Connections. Painting by Zeno Diemer.
     Courtesy: Deutsches Museum, München   92

23. Aqua Claudia "arcus neroniani"
     Courtesy: Fototeca Unione 851   94

24. Forum of Augustus, Rome
     Courtesy: Fototeca Unione 447   110

25. Chart 3. Harbor of Ostia
     Source: M. K. and R. L. Thornton   146

---

*Reprinted with permission of Macmillan Publishing Company from *ANCIENT HISTORY ATLAS* by Michael Grant. Copyright © 1971 by Macmillan Publishing Company.
†Fototeca Unione at the American Academy in Rome.

The following labels appear on the map:

BRITANNIA

LWR. GERMANY (17 B.C.)

FREE GERMANY

Temporarily conquered from 15 B.C. but abandoned after ambushing of Varus by Arminius in A.D. 9

Colonia Agrippinensis

Rhine

Moguntiacum

Danube

LOWER PANNON

BELGICA

LUGDUNENSIS

UPR. GERMANY (17 B.C.)

RHAETIA (15 B.C.)

NORICUM (15 B.C.)

UPPER PANNONIA

Lugdunum

Aquileia

AQUITANIA

P

C

NARBONENSIS

M

ITALY

Adriatic Sea

Nemausus

Rome

TARRACONENSIS

Tarraco

LUSITANIA (c. 27 B.C.)

Corduba

BAETICA

Gades

Naulochus

SICILY

Carthage

Naval victory Sextus Pompe 36 B.C.

MAURETANIA

AFRIC

Legend:

━━━━ Imperial frontier as in A.D. 14

– – – – Provincial frontiers

ASIA Senatorial provinces

ALPINE PROVINCES (15-14 B.C.)
M: Maritime, C: Cottian, P: Pennine

The hatched areas represent the more important dependent ('client') states, whose monarchs enjoyed internal autonomy but had to support Rome's foreign policy and help defend the imperial frontiers.

///// Principal client states

The Roman Empire at the Time of Augustus, A.D. 14.

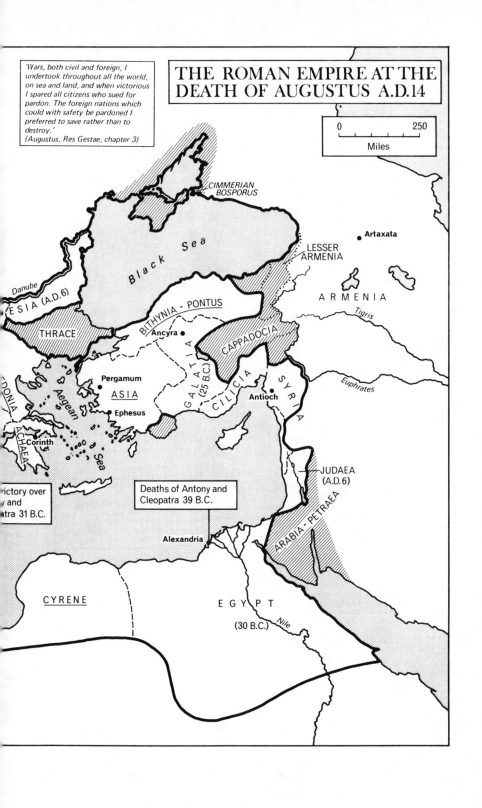

'Wars, both civil and foreign, I undertook throughout all the world, on sea and land, and when victorious I spared all citizens who sued for pardon. The foreign nations which could with safety be pardoned I preferred to save rather than to destroy.'
(Augustus, Res Gestae, chapter 3)

THE ROMAN EMPIRE AT THE DEATH OF AUGUSTUS A.D.14

0   250

Miles

CIMMERIAN BOSPORUS

Artaxata

Black Sea

LESSER ARMENIA

ARMENIA

Danube

ESIA (A.D.6)

Tigris

THRACE

BITHYNIA - PONTUS

Ancyra

CAPPADOCIA

Pergamum

GALATIA (25 B.C.)

CILICIA

SYRIA

Euphrates

Antioch

ASIA

Aegean Sea

Ephesus

DONIA

ACHAEA

Corinth

JUDAEA (A.D.6)

Deaths of Antony and Cleopatra 39 B.C.

ARABIA - PETRAEA

ictory over
y and
tra 31 B.C.

Alexandria

CYRENE

EGYPT

(30 B.C.)

Nile

JULIO-CLAUDIAN BUILDING PROGRAMS:

A Quantitative Study in Political Management

I. INTRODUCTION[1]

Before Augustus acquired the *imperium* in 27 B.C., Rome was basically an Italic nation. Had she fragmented into several pieces with the demise of the Republic, her place in history might have been modest. She, however, did not. Instead she evolved into a positive agent of human development, the central power in the Mediterranean region whose overwhelming contribution was the provision of political stability.

We are concerned here with establishing the interrelationships between governmental actions and the general economic environment. We have limited our concern, however, to one narrow segment of the transition, that involving the specific changes which had to be made within the city of Rome itself: the toga of power which the city had to don to take her place as administrative center for the empire. In the process of becoming an empire, Rome had to discard her old traditions: she could do this because the problems arising from her civil wars and their accompanying insecurity had been solved. The city no longer needed to feed itself: it paid for its imports by exporting good government and Pax Romana.

Obviously growth was inevitable, not just in numbers of inhabitants, but in their quality of life. This meant major construction in a variety of forms. The Julio-Claudian emperors, inheriting the task of managing physical growth, used their building programs as a principal tool for meeting Rome's needs—that is, as a means of satisfying the physical and the psychological needs of the recently founded empire. The Julio-Claudians had, of course, to construct temples, basilicas and monuments; new dynasties need such psychological proof of power.[2] Even more important they had to meet the city's physical needs: to feed it, to furnish it water, and to provide it with the means of human enjoyment.

The need for these amenities of life did not suddenly arise; Rome did not grow from an Italic power to be a Mediterranean one overnight. She gained much of the South shore of the Mediterranean with the Third Punic War (146 B.C.) and when Augustus finally defeated his rivals, Cleopatra, the Queen of Egypt,

3

and her Roman ally, Antony, in 31 B.C. She obtained the North
Central shore when Corinth, standard bearer of the Greek States,
was annihilated in 146 B.C.; she further consolidated the East
when she annexed Pergamum into the Province of Asia in 129
B.C. On the West, she subdued Spain by 133 B.C. On the North,
Rome's defeat of Vercingetorix in 51 B.C. marked the end of
independent Gaul. While she contended with continuous muti-
nies, skirmishes, forcible demonstrations, and border clashes on
the fringes of the Empire, she had no armed threats to the safety
of the core of the empire after about 13 B.C. when Illyricum
ceased to be a problem.[3]

From a Roman building point of view the key result of these
conquests was to allow Rome to grow into an imperial city. There
was no longer any credible military threat from a foreign power.
Rome's planners could cater to the living comforts of the inhabitants of the city. Her architects could now build for gracious
living.

Although the city planner still needed political developments
to free his hands to his task and to provide continuity of control
over the city's future, he also needed a long period for plans to
jell and for the necessary resources to be gathered together if he
were to complete major projects. The years between the con-
quest of the Mediterranean and between the development of
political stability were the years of the Roman Revolution, a
period in which the Romans decided the shape of Roman Government by fighting it out on the battlefield. When the Augustan
forces finally won out at Actium (31 B.C.), the Julio-Claudians
had gained the conditions necessary for the Roman Government
to build a magnificent city. As Frank C. Bourne notes: "To a
man of vision there was a great need to create a city worthy to
be an imperial capital, *urbs pro majestate imperii ornata.*"[4]

Among Augustus' first imperial acts were the ritualistic,
public-relations ones of building or of repairing political symbols
such as temples and monuments. Further, the last years of the
Republic were chaotic: since central administration was inse-
cure, maintenance and upkeep of the existing infrastructure (temple, for example) had been allowed to deteriorate markedly.[5]
While these building projects were highly visible, undoubtedly
necessary to support a still shaky power position and essential
to provide religious legitimacy to the new regime, they were not
usually very expensive in terms of manpower or of materials
costs. The new emperor had to focus as the central theme of his

regime on the more basic human needs for food, for an adequate water supply, and for recreation facilities for a large and restless urban population. In other words, the Julio-Claudian emperors had to make it possible for the Roman citizen to eat, to drink, and to be merry.

EAT

As Rome grew in population, she needed an ever increasing supply of wheat. She had long depended heavily on overseas sources for her food. According to Josephus, Egypt in the Early Empire provided nearly one-third of Rome's grain needs and Africa, nearly two-thirds (*BJ* 2.383; 386). Rome could generally depend on such overseas sources to provide sufficient grain to meet her needs; the problem, however, was primarily one of seeing that the grain reached the city in sufficient quantity and with regularity to prevent food shortages. There had been a very serious famine with an accompanying riot in 57 B.C.[6] Almost immediately upon the establishment of the Principate, Augustus had to solve a serious food crisis; since he was never able to solve the food problem totally, he left his successors with famine as a continuous worry. Augustus met his specific crises in various ways: He tells us that on numerous occasions he gave grain to the people (*Res Gestae* 5, 15 & 18). Some believe that he was even involved in planning for a harbor at Ostia by which action he would better be able to keep a constant flow of grain coming to Rome. Carcopino believes that the death of Agrippa prevented Augustus from carrying out the project.[7] We know that in 23 B.C. the emperor allocated to Tiberius the task of moving the corn up the Tiber to Rome (Suet. *Tib.* 8). When Tiberius as the quaestor was unable to resolve the problem of famine, Augustus considered it so serious a problem that he himself, taking charge of the grain-supply temporarily, freed the people from fear of hunger.[8] There can be no question that the food supply was a vital part of Augustus' political policy. It was essential that solutions to this problem would underlie a major segment of his public works program.

DRINK

Augustus was already involved in solving his water supply problems before the Principate had even been established. In 33 B.C. Agrippa, his colleague, was already deeply preoccupied with cleaning up and repairing the dilapidated Republican aqueducts.

During the Civil War there had been no systematic maintenance of the aqueducts; consequently, the conduits had been damaged due to the construction of tombs and of roads over them and due to the action of the roots of trees planted too close to them. Even the repairmen who attempted to perform repairs were hindered by local landlords who were stealing water for their own private irrigation schemes (Front. *Aq.* 2.125–126). Augustus needed the aqueducts to be in good repair not only for the provision of necessary water but also for the beautification of the city. To show that water was a concern of his, Augustus carefully stated in his propaganda-oriented *Res Gestae* (see below) that he restored the channels which had lacked maintenance for many years and doubled the channel of the Aqua Marcia by turning a new spring into its channel (Front. *Aq.* 2.125). In addition, he built two other aqueducts, the Aqua Alsietina and the Aqua Virgo.

. . . AND BE MERRY

The third of the three requirements facing Augustus was a psychological one stemming from the disruptions of the late Republic. The formation and subsequent disbandment of the several contending armies had created a mass of formerly rural ex-soldiers, too long absent from their farms and too unskilled to secure other employment. While many of them stayed in rural locations, still a large number of these potentially troublesome indigents migrated into the City itself. Republican leaders had refused to provide their discharged soldiers with either land or a discharge bonus. As a result, "the rural poor—tenants, agricultural laborers, and small farmers—filled the ranks of the army, creating a potentially explosive force. An increased urban violence has often been pointed to as a prime factor in the demise of the free state."[9] Augustus, for the peace of the city, had to provide them with either land or money,[10] or with jobs (one of the theses of this research), and with something to keep their minds off their troubles—to make merry. He implemented construction programs that provided the Roman population with baths, with circuses and with theaters.

OBJECTIVES

We intend through this research to develop an understanding of the economic conditions in the Early Empire. Our literary sources are limited. First, only a small part of Roman literature

dealing with the history of the Roman Empire from 27 B.C. to
A.D. 68, the chronological period involved in this study, has
survived. For this period the basic works are: one Cassius Dio's
History, of which the extant portion runs from before our period
to A.D. 46; a second, the extant books of the *Annals* of Tacitus
which cover the reign of Tiberius (14–37), the last seven years
of Claudius (47–54) and the first twelve years of Nero (54–66).
The gaps in the *Annals* include the reign of Gaius (Caligula), a
period of almost four years from A.D. 37–41 and the first six
years of Claudius' reign (41–47); the third, the *Lives of the Cae-
sars,* written by the biographer Suetonius, covers the reigns from
Augustus to Nero; in other words, all the emperors included in
this study.

In assessing the value of these three sources, we must keep
in mind that only one of these writers, Tacitus, was a contemporary of the Julio-Claudians; he was, however, only fourteen
when Nero the last Julio-Claudian died.[11] He would, in addition
to written and oral narratives and anecdotes of the general history
of the period, have had available to him such sources of information as: *acta senatus* (the published record of the proceedings
of the senate), *acta populi* (a court journal that contained the
same type of reporting as that found in a modern newspaper),
and the private journals of the emperors.[12]

A second source was Suetonius, born around A.D. 75, a time
shortly after our period. As the Emperor Hadrian's private secretary in A.D. 119–121, he is chronologically still close enough
to the Julio-Claudian emperors to have used some of the same
sources.

The third source, Dio, is writing at the end of the 2nd century
A.D. and the beginning of the 3rd century, a time well after our
period.

The writers differ in their purpose in writing. Tacitus tells
us in his own words: "I think that it is the special duty of an
historian to extol virtues and to give base words and deeds a
fear of future infamy" (*Ann.* 3.65.1). He longs for the good old
days which were "the earliest age of mankind" (*Ann.* 3.26.1).
He clearly believes that the teaching of his morality is important.
Syme notes that Dio is a "fervent advocate of the monarchial
rule."[13] Suetonius, on the other hand, has little use for morality.
He is exceedingly interested in gossip and any new scandal.

The inscription *Res Gestae* furnishes us another ancient
source. It is a self-written record of Augustus' career preserved

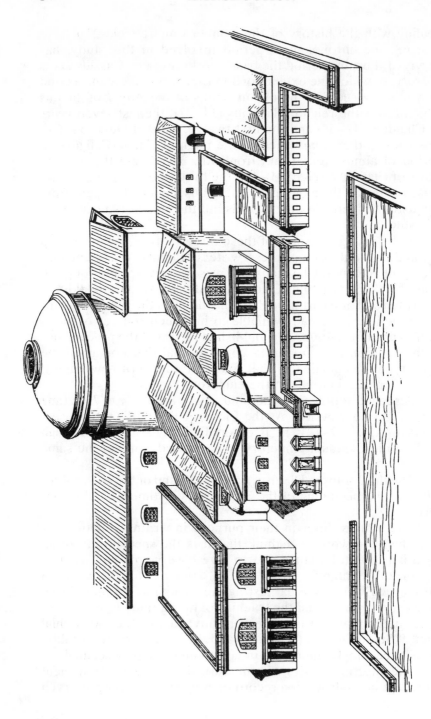

Reconstruction of Thermae of Agrippa (from Hülsen, 1910)

Thermae of Agrippa in the via della Ciambella

for us in copies chiselled on the walls of the Temple of Rome and Augustus in Asia Minor. Two copies are present: one in Greek, one in Latin.

The ancient historians might differ in purpose but they had certain subjects in which they had an interest: politics and war. Manpower or economics did not concern them unless it directly involved politics or war as it did in the financial crisis of A.D. 33.

Consequently, we find the literary sources are of restricted value on the issues of interest to this study. They seem to assume that there are no variations in the environment. To them, since working people always work, there is no need for labor to concern itself with changes in its employment. It takes little research to discover that there must have been major changes: soldiers were recruited; wars were fought; major labor-using projects were started and different projects were completed. Since the common man obviously had to change his job, there were surely at different times a larger or smaller number of alternative employments for him to choose from—either on his own or through his owner.

We hope here not only to shed some light on the demand for labor during the period but also to illuminate overall economic conditions. We limit our effort, however, to the city of Rome itself and to a radius of 60 kilometers from the city center. Our choice of limits is, first, to restrict an already ambitious study to an area for which public construction projects have been well-documented. On the other hand, we want to expand the range to cover all the region which logically should have been one unitary labor market, that is, one in which labor would have moved freely from job to job.

We extend our outer limits to cover the sources of aqueducts where they are more than 60 kilometers from the city; further, because labor forces almost certainly interchanged with Claudius' force which drained the Fucine Lake, we include that project as a special study. In addition, we treat in a separate chapter the building of the harbor of Ostia. Although that port city is within the 60 kilometer radius of our study, it is so different in its requirements, in the quality of data available and in the kind of labor involved as to demand special treatment.

We further limit our study to public building programs although the vast majority of constructions in Rome was private. Since the populace lived in the numerous *insulae*, a large portion of the labor force was undoubtedly engaged in the construction of these apartment-houses. It would be difficult to attempt a quantification of this work. Numbers of *insulae* are in doubt; there are problems in making the number predicted fit on the available acreage, and loss rates through fire and through collapse were quite high.[14] There are, unfortunately, almost no sources which cover private building comprehensively; we do know that James E. Packer in his study of Seneca (*Ben.* 4.6.2; 6.15.7; *Ira* 3.35.4–5) has reported that "the apartment houses of Rome were insubstantial structures, and his (Seneca's) works are full of metaphors drawn from the cracking, collapsing, or burning of these buildings."[15] Strabo, Augustus' contemporary, stresses the insecurity of the construction with its constant threat of fire and collapse (Strabo, 235). In an attempt to alleviate the unsafe housing conditions, Augustus limited the height of the buildings in the city to 70 feet; his efforts seem to have been in vain since the Romans were still complaining in Nero's time. We have not attempted, therefore, a quantification of private building.

We do not feel that lack of knowledge of private building limits the value of our study. The doyens of macro-economics, Joseph Schumpeter and J. M. Keynes, support our belief that public building is a dependable indicator of the general state of an economy.[16]

Schumpeter explains the general business cycle as dependent on waves of innovation in "narrow but important segments" of an economy; both of the Julio-Claudian major public building programs (one before 12 B.C., the other from A.D. 37 to A.D. 68), separated as they are by about 50 years, meet Schumpeter's concept of waves of innovation in a "narrow but important" segment. Keynes' theory of periods of prosperity and depression partially depends directly on cycles of public spending; again his necessary conditions existed during the Julio-Claudian period.

We still face the problem of the degrees to which public and private building occurred simultaneously. It would be possible that the private building which resulted from the public building programs lagged behind significantly. The hypothesis that private building took over where public building left off is a persuasive one. If we presume that public building is the engine that drives the private economy, we can suggest that labor was attracted into (or directed into) the city for public construction work. The need to house this new labor force fueled a secondary boom in private housing which employed the original labor as public construction tapered off. In his economic survey Tenney Frank thinks that the Augustan peace on land and sea, the protection of private property, the unusual expansion of coinage and the free spending of state funds on public works, all made for a period of prosperity during which Rome expanded rapidly and erected a vast number of private buildings.[17] He suggests, however, that the "Augustan Prosperity" was congruent with Augustus' building programs rather than a follow-on to them. If this is true—Tenney Frank's supporting citations are not strong—then private building would have enhanced the cycle rather than reduced it.[18]

Conceptually, it is obvious that private building would follow very closely on public building: workmen were in the city; they would need shelter and other support.[19]

Since our objective is to determine periods of high demand and of low demand for labor, the private building of the time will be principally an addition to the public picture. Its main effect would be possibly to lengthen the demand for labor for a time after the public building slacked off to provide housing for the workers, still sleeping in the streets or in tents.

MANAGERIAL ANALYSIS

A more diffuse objective of our study is to gain insight into the managerial sophistication of the rulers responsible for approving and for carrying out the building programs. We hope to estimate the degree to which projects undertaken were a result of broad, long-range plans phased against capabilities and started against a logical priority list. We hope to integrate what is known of the personal attributes of each Emperor into our own estimate of the logic behind each project set. We hope to compare needs to personality, availabilities to the need for public support, politics to logic.

If we are successful in this effort, we believe that we will be able to distill from the conclusions a greater understanding of the degree to which in Roman times men made history rather than history making men.

ENDNOTES TO CHAPTER I

[1]Portions of this chapter appeared in the article "Julio-Claudian Building Programs: Eat, Drink and Be Merry" by M. K. Thornton in *Historia* 35 (1986), 28–44.

[2]For examples, see Paul MacKendrick, *The Mute Stones Speak* (New York, 1960), 117; 136; 143.

[3]Ronald Syme, "Some Notes on the Legions under Augustus," *JRS* 23 (1933), 22–23.

[4]F. C. Bourne, *Public Works of the Julio-Claudians* (Princeton, N.J., 1941), 1.

[5]D. E. Strong, "The Administration of Public Building in Rome During the Late Republic and Early Empire," *Institute of Classical Studies Bulletin* 15 (1968), 103; Cf. Dio 49, 16.

[6]Cic. *De Imp. Pomp.* 44; Plut. *Pomp.* 27.2.; Erich S. Gruen, *The Last Generation of the Roman Republic* (Berkeley, Los Angeles, London, 1974), 436.

[7]Jerome Carcopino, *Ostie* (Paris, 1929), 738.

[8]Dio 54.1.3; *Res Gestae* 5.2.

[9]Gruen, *The Last Generation of the Roman Republic*, 358.

[10]He settled dischargees with allotments of land or with cash bounties: P.A. Brunt, "The Army and the Land in the Roman Revolution," *JRS* 52 (1962), 84.

[11]The exact date of the birth of Tacitus is not known. Henry Furneaux suggests A.D. 54 in *The Annals of Tacitus* (Oxford, 1965), 2nd edition, 2).

[12]For more information on the sources of Tacitus, see Furneaux, *Annals*, 13–22; Ronald Syme, *Tacitus* (Oxford, 1958), 271–303).

[13]*Tacitus*, 272.

[14]G. Hermansen, "Domus and Insula in the City of Rome," *Classica et Mediaevalia* (Copenhagen, 1973), 333–337.

[15]"Housing and Population in Imperial Ostia and Rome," *JRS* 57 (1967), 80.

[16]Joseph Schumpeter, *Business Cycles* (New York, 1939), *passim* and J.M. Keynes, *The General Theory of Employment Interest and Money* (New York, 1935), *passim*.

[17]*ESAR*, V (Baltimore, 1940), 19–20.

[18]Cf. with M. K. Thornton, "Augustan Tradition and Neronian Economics," *ANRW* II.2, 149–171.

[19]Cf. Henry C. Boren, "The Urban Side of the Gracchan Economic Crisis," *American Historical Review* 63 (1958), 895–6.

II. MANPOWER COSTS OF THE BUILDING PROGRAMS

The core of research around which we constructed this book is a project by project evaluation of all the public works programs from 29 B.C. to A.D. 68 within our target geographical area.[1] The dates, of course, cover the entire Julio-Claudian dynasty, from Augustus through Tiberius, Caligula (Gaius), Claudius, to Nero. Our focus is on labor demands; thus, our concentration is on assessing the relative labor requirements needed to complete each of the projects identified. To the maximum extent possible we assign each project to a specific year or years; thus, we will have on completion a year by year demand schedule for manpower.

We will do the research in three phases: in the first phase we determine the relative manpower cost of each separate building project performed in the targeted place and period. In the second phase we summarize the resultant cost figures by year and chart them to develop a pattern. In the third phase we consider alternative explanations for the resulting cyclical pattern.

DETERMINATION OF MANPOWER COST

Our first task is to identify the relevant public building; our second, to assign a relative manpower cost to each separate project.

Identification of Projects

We include all identifiable public building projects started or completed from 29 B.C. until A.D. 68 in an area within 60 kilometers of Rome as the locus of investigation. Within such a range the labor force would be mobile and contractors from Rome might be expected to bid for work. If we enlarge the radius significantly the only important problem which will arise is the inclusion of the Fucine Lake project. We treat this large project later.

Once we had determined the time frame of building projects and the geographic range of buildings, we used literary and archaeological sources to identify the specific projects. The main

15

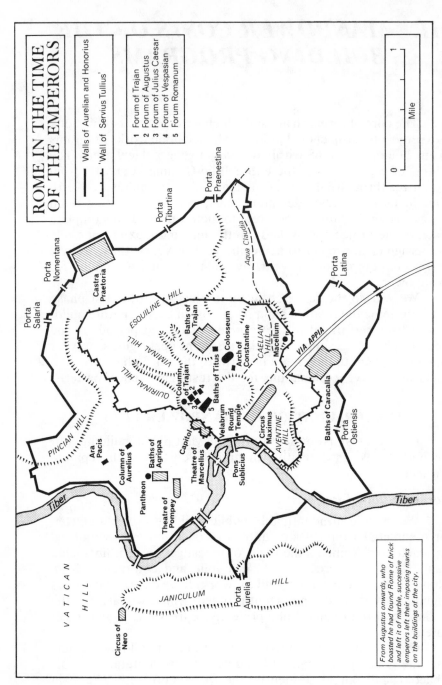

ROME IN THE TIME OF THE EMPERORS

—— Walls of Aurelian and Honorius
········· 'Wall of Servius Tullius'

1 Forum of Trajan
2 Forum of Augustus
3 Forum of Julius Caesar
4 Forum of Vespasian
5 Forum Romanum

0 ———————— 1
      Mile

Porta Nomentana
Porta Salaria
Castra Praetoria
Porta Tiburtina
Porta Praenestina
ESQUILINE HILL
VIMINAL HILL
QUIRINAL HILL
PINCIAN HILL
Baths of Trajan
Colosseum
Arch of Constantine
CAELIAN HILL
Macellum
Column of Trajan
Baths of Titus
Round Temple
Velabrum
Circus Maximus
AVENTINE HILL
Baths of Caracalla
Porta Ostiensis
VIA APPIA
Porta Latina
Aqua Claudia
Ara Pacis
Column of Aurelius
Pantheon
Baths of Agrippa
Theatre of Pompey
Capitol
Theatre of Marcellus
Pons Sublicius
Tiber
VATICAN HILL
Circus of Nero
JANICULUM HILL
Porta Aurelia

From Augustus onwards, who boasted he had found Rome of brick and left it of marble, successive emperors left their imposing marks on the buildings of the city.

Rome in the Time of the Emperors

Maison Carrée (Nîmes, France)

secondary sources were Platner-Ashby, for the identification of projects in and around the city, and Frontinus, supplemented by Ashby and Van Deman for the study of aqueducts.[2]

We undoubtedly missed some projects in a period of nearly a century during which time the emperors created a great city, transformed from one of brick to one of marble (Suet. *Aug*. 28.3). But archaeologists have recorded few finds not mentioned in the literary sources, suggesting that literary sources are reliable; literary references, on the other hand, exist for buildings leaving no trace in the archaeology. The possible conclusion—that most sizeable projects appear somewhere in the literature even without archaeological evidence—is reassuring. Had this not been so, we might have omitted significant projects and their manpower costs.

Archaeology, with its definable dimensions, nonetheless makes an essential contribution. Augustus in his *Res Gestae* shows us the pitfalls of a wholly literary method by his unequal recording of projects in different time periods. Augustus, covert breaker of tradition that he was, took pains to list his building accomplishments in great detail. Justification was politically important to the first emperor; his *Res Gestae* lists in bronze throughout the Empire his building accomplishments (Suet. *Aug*. 101). If we merely count the number of his imperial building projects, we might believe that he did a large amount of construction; if, however, we examine the type of projects we find out that many of Augustus' works, consisting as they do of minor constructions, have, on quantifying, trivial impact on manpower demands. There remains an Augustan spurt in building but it was not the major event that a reading of *Res Gestae* undisciplined by quantification might suggest.

Of course, there are a fair number of projects listed in literary sources for which there are significant (unquantifiable) data on size and on effort plus insufficient physical remains left to allow us to make an accurate assessment of relative manpower costs. In such cases, we reckon the project as average in size for its type. While the guesses can be high or quite low in each case, the errors should roughly cancel out in aggregate.

Particularly during the earlier years of the Empire, it is sometimes unclear whether a building is public. The study does not cover unquestionably private buildings. However, we were uncertain as to the classification of a group of projects intended for public use but erected or maintained by private funds. We considered buildings to be public when the private funds were unquestionably those of the emperor or his immediate family. Where a private family funded the work as in the rebuilding of the Basilica Aemilia, facts were more inconclusive. On the whole, we accepted the opinion of previous researchers; if a project was listed among public works by such authorities as Platner-Ashby, we considered it public.

Individual Project Evaluation

We adopt the use of index numbers as our approach to quantification. We select one type of building as the base, expressing all other construction as a ratio between the amount of work required to do it and the base.

For example, if the base were taken to be 60 work units (WU), then a building taking twice the effort would require 120 WUs, one needing but half the work would be rated at 30 WUs. The base work's number is wholly arbitrary; it bears no necessary relationship to man-hours, work-days, or other physical units of work.

In determining the work unit allocation, we include all necessary operations taking place within the area covered by the study. All stone quarrying, mason work, earth movement, artistic embellishment, carpentry and transport within the area are taken to be part of the project. Relative money costs between, say, marble and tufa were not considered except to the degree that the composition of the different materials made fabrication more or less difficult.

Indexing Approach

The authors after considerable thought chose to use an index method of measurement rather than one based on an absolute work unit, such as a man-day. We had two primary considerations: first, it is difficult to secure acceptable absolute data on work performed in, say, man-days in grossly different tooling environments. For example, one of the authors was involved in reviewing construction work done exclusively with hand tools under primitive conditions in Burma during 1945–46. Without power tools the skill requirements on the worker are very different from those with which the modern engineers are familiar. Skills used by less well tooled artisans took decades to develop; modern time and motion studies would have been inappropriate since no modern artisan would possess the needed but long obsolete skills. Estimates of absolute man-days used would have been subject to gross errors. On the other hand, the relative approach adopted here is less dubious; all that is needed is the assumption that skills and methods used on one project are the same as those used on compared ones.

The possibility of error in the number of man-days was but one consideration supporting an approach using relative index numbers. The definition of the study demanded only the degree of *variability* in work done over the time period under study; it demanded only relative judgments. Indeed, a study expressed in absolute terms would have had little relevance (except to compare through relatives again) without far greater quantification of the entire society than can ever be expected.

We made an effort to use the absolute sesterces value of construction as provided by Richard Duncan-Jones to provide comparisons between different types of buildings.[3] The effort was not successful primarily because of the inadequate information available.

The use of index numbers avoids a serious problem which worried us for some time: the problem of the depth of infrastructure which we should include in our project costs. A temple may have included in its costs its "on site" manpower costs, or might also include, for example, the cost of making its bricks, or the costs of transporting them to the site, or even of digging the original clay from which the bricks are made; shall we add in the kiln firewood costs? All estimates of manpower needs must deal with deciding which functions are to be included, which are deemed to be "bought out." In all cases in any time or place the quoted figure is commonly accepted as made "according to the customs of the industry." Our use of index numbers recognizes the total inadequacy of a "man-hour" figure in a wholly different commercial situation. It carries the warning, however, that even our index number approach presumes that all of the compared projects are performed in similar industrial environments. Within the city and its environs we feel such a presumption is justified. We will discuss it further when we talk about the work done in the draining of the Fucine Lake.

Work Unit Base

We base the work unit on the amount of work believed to be needed to build anew the Maison Carrée at Nîmes (16 B.C.). This temple seems a logical choice to use as a basic unit because, according to Banister Fletcher, it "is the best preserved Roman temple in existence, and is externally complete. It represents the ultimate of Graeco-Etruscan design interpreted in monumental Augustan architecture."[4]

This temple is *arbitrarily* set at *60* work units (WU). Its size is 32 m. × 15 m.;[5] it occupies 480 m² of ground space; thus, 1 WU is used to construct, to this temple's standards, 8 m² of temple (floor space area). We consider that temples of unknown dimensions were average temples to which we assigned 100 work units, a reasonable average relative to 60 since the Maison Carrée (60 work units) is a small temple. We compared all other measurements of work units to the Maison Carrée standard.

The use of square meters of floor space as a basis seems a valid one since even today a contractor states the cost of building in areal terms; for instance, he bases house-building cost-estimates on floor area. The more square feet, the more expensive the house. As a Roman example Cato (*RR* 14.3) remarks that the cost of the building for an owner providing the materials should be one sesterce per roof-tile, another areal measure.[6]

Using the Nîmes temple as our basic unit, we need to consider other data such as: (1) What was the degree of elaboration of the construction (obtained from archaeological and literary sources)? (2) What were the measurements of the building (from archaeological sources)? (3) What was done to the building? We use different percentages for the type of work done. For example, the construction of a new building received 1.00 of its full value in work units but the restoration of an old building might take but 40 percent. For other types of work done on a building different factors were allowed. We made modifications to the factors based on specific information from the sources.

In determining the kind of work done, we adopted tentatively the verb used by the most authoritative source available, e.g., "rebuilds," "dedicates," "enlarges." We then checked the work done from whatever added data was available; archaeological and other sources permit further refinements. We can show an example of our methodology, when we determined the WU value of restoring the Temple of Magna Mater:

Augustus in 3 A.D. restored the Temple of Magna Mater (*PA*, 594 and 324). Its extant remains are practically non-existent. Its size was 33m × 17m = 561m². When we divided 561 by 8 to adjust it to our standard unit, the temple of Maison Carrée, we found it to be 70 WUs:

$$561m^2 \div 8m^2 = 70 \text{ WUs}.$$

Since the temple was not built as a new building but was a restoration, we multiplied the measurement by .4 (factor assigned for restorations):

$$70 \text{ WUs} \times .4 = 28 \text{ WUs}$$

(assigned to this construction). Blake asserts that "The burning of the Temple of Magna Mater on the Palatine in A.D. 3 was not serious enough to injure the statue of Claudia in its vestibule (Valerius Max. 1.8.11). Consequently, it is difficult to tell how extensive the Augustan restoration was. Apparently Augustus did sufficient work on it so that he felt justified in listing it among the temples rebuilt by him (Aug. *Res Gestae* 19)."[7]

Such a conclusion as Blake drew seems to justify our assigning only .4 to a restoration. Had the burning been serious enough to injure the statue of Claudia, we might have changed our tentative "restore" (.4) to "rebuild" (.6).

The verbs used in the research and their factor value are as follows:

Verb	Percentage of value in WU (as a factor)
1. Builds	1.0
2. Erects	.8
3. Reclaims	.7
4. Rebuilds	.6
5. Enlarges	.5
6. Extends	.5
7. Restores	.4
8. Repairs (aqueduct)	.2
9. Dedicates	.1
10. Founds	.1
11. Gives	.1
12. Vows	.1
13. Removes	.1

Quality of Construction

Different types of construction would require, of course, more or less labor per square meter. Since a temple is more ornate than some other buildings, our study requires the following adjustments: we gave a basilica, also ornate, the same work units as a temple; all lower grade administrative buildings, however, we valued as half of a temple unit. For instance, Juvenal (*Sat.* 6.529) speaks of the Saepta Julia as a mere *ovile*, a sheepfold; Middleton describes it as "an immensely long covered porticus or rectangular building supported by rows of piers, forming seven parallel lines of aisles."[8] It was a large building (its measurements were 300m × 95m = 28,500m²) but austere.[9] Its measurements of 28,500m² were divided by 8 (the number of work units per m² obtained by dividing the square footage of the floor plan of the Maison Carrée by 60, the number of work units arbitrarily assigned to Maison Carrée) to adjust it to the basic unit:

$$28,500m^2 \div 8 = 3563 \text{ WUs.}$$

The 3563, in turn, was multiplied by .5 (the rate for a lower grade building):

$$3563 \text{ WUs} \times .5 = 1782 \text{ WUs.}$$

Since a portion of the work on the Saepta Julia was done before our beginning date (Dio 53.23), we divided the last figure by 3, presuming that two-thirds of the work was done before and one-third after our starting date:

$$1782 \div 3 = 594 \text{ WUs.}$$

An explanation of the system for assigning values to three other important construction types (*domus*, aqueducts, and theaters) is found in Appendix 1.

Assignment of Construction Dates

Chronological dating is the next important task of the research. Because determination of annual public works burdens is a central objective of the research, we need to assign projects to specific calendar years. Because some projects are quite large, we felt the need to spread their construction over several years. Sometimes the sources give beginning and completion dates as in the following:

7 B.C.—A.D. 10. Temple of Concord started in 7 B.C. and finished in A.D. 10 (Dio 55.8.2; 56.55)

21 A.D.—A.D. 41. Theater of Pompey burned; work started by Tiberius, finished under Caligula or Claudius (Dio 60.6)

A.D. 38—52. Aquae Claudia and Anio Novus built (Front. *Aq.*, 1.13)

In most cases, however, we do not find the dates of constructions conveniently stated. Sometimes we know only when a building was dedicated. Where a specific date of beginning and ending are given for a large project, we spread the work units, depending on the size of the projects, over a number of years. For example, in the case of temples, if there are no definite dates for a given one, we make an allocation, based on Blake's research on temples. Blake has listed a number of temples with the dates representing the interval between the vow and the dedication of the finished temple: some temples took 10 years to build; others, only one.[10]

We usually assigned three years to a temple whose start and finish are unknown. Again, if a project, dated to one year, seemed too large for the allotted time and no literary reference suggests the contrary, we spread its time of construction over several years. We dated other projects only as belonging to the reign of a certain emperor. We added together the work units of all such constructions and divided them by the number of years of the reign to get an annual average; then we spread this average evenly throughout the reign. The total work units treated so were not large.

RESEARCH RESULTS

Our quantification of the building activities of the Julio-Claudian emperors permits us to make some useful observations. We discover that in this period a project, unless large, has little impact on a building program or on the economy. This observation is important because it flows from our results *at the crudest level*. Furthermore, we show that *Res Gestae* type propaganda can easily be supplanted by the type of study that we have done. One of the advantages gained from this type of systematic study is that definite findings are confirmed even by *gross* results. Consequently, the only constructions that might affect a cyclical trend are the key building projects listed in the chart below.

Chart of Key Building Projects

Building	Time in Construction	Type of Work	Work Units Assigned
1. Saepta Julia	29–26 B.C.	Started earlier by Caesar, continued by Lepidus, dedicated by Augustus	594
2. Thermae Agrippae	25–21 B.C.	Built	1125

3. Aqua Virgo	24–19 B.C.	Completed	2295
4. Theater of Marcellus	17–13 B.C.	Built	2208
5. Theater of Balbus	17–13 B.C.	Built	1709
6. Diribitorium	11–7 B.C.	Built	394
7. Aqueducts	11–4 B.C.	Restored	8487
8. Alsietina Aqueduct	11–4 B.C.	Constructed	3281
9. Forum of Augustus	3–2 B.C.	Built	580
10. Basilica Julia	A.D. 9–12	Rebuilt & enlarged	495
11. Aqua Julia	A.D. 14	Restored	913
12. Domus Tiberiana (1)	A.D. 14–37	Built	1350
13. Castra Praetoria	A.D. 22–23	Built	804
14. Theater of Pompey	A.D. 21–37	Restored	673
15. Domus Tiberiana (2)	A.D. 37–41	Extended	1350
16. Aqua Claudia	A.D. 38–52	Built	6868
17. Aqua Anio Novus	A.D. 38–52	Built	8688
18. Domus Transitoria	A.D. 55–61	Built	1000
19. Thermae Neronianae	A.D. 62–64	Built	2850
20. Domus Aurea	A.D. 65–68	Built	2000
21. House of Vestals	A.D. 65–67	Rebuilt	618

Specifications on all projects, totalling 178, are recorded in Appendix 2.

Next, we charted the information collected on all 178 constructions (see Chart 1, Chapt. 2 and its data sheet). Two major and two minor peaks of building activity stand out. The highest peak is the Augustan boom between 12 B.C. and 3 B.C. The following projects, each with at least 350 WUs, were responsible for the peak:

Restorations of the aqueducts	(11–4 B.C.)	8487
Construction of Aqua Alsietina	(11–4 B.C.)	3281
Seven barracks for Cohortes Vigilium	(10–8 B.C.)	360
Diribitorium	(11–7 B.C.)	394
Forum of Augustus	(3–2 B.C.)	580

The other major peak was between A.D. 38–51; it was basically caused by extensive aqueduct building. The main projects were:

Extensions of Domus Tiberiana (2)	(A.D. 37–41)	1350
Building of the Aqua Claudia	(A.D. 38–52)	6868
Building of the Anio Novus	(A.D. 38–52)	8688
Restoration of Aqua Virgo	(A.D. 46–54)	918

Of the two minor peaks, the highest occurred between A.D. 61–68. The constructions during that time were:

Domus Transitoria	(A.D. 55–61)	1000
Thermae Neronianae	(A.D. 62–64)	2850
Domus Aurea	(A.D. 65–68)	2000
House of Vestals	(A.D. 65–67)	618

The other minor peak occurred from 22–12 B.C.; the projects then were:

Thermae Agrippae	(25–21 B.C.)	1125
Aqua Virgo	(24–19 B.C.)	2295
Theater of Marcellus	(17–13 B.C.)	2208
Theater of Balbus	(17–13 B.C.)	1709

The peak of the first major cycle occurs in 7 B.C.; that of the second, in A.D. 38. This provides an intervening period of 46 years. Modern macro-economic theorists have studied business cycles in some depth and have analyzed them into separate sets of naturally occurring cycles; some are of long duration from prosperity through recession to prosperity; others are of short duration. Interestingly, the long waves of the Kondratieff cycle, important to modern macro-economic theory, have an average period of 50–60 years, while the minor interim one, the Juglar cycle, has from 9 to 10 years.[11] An evaluation of the causes of the intensive concentration of work in these two high points makes it clear that they result from two strongly pursued water supply projects; aqueduct building creates these peaks.

Since aqueduct projects were very significant in forming the peaks in Roman building cycles, we decided to review the details by which we assigned work units to aqueducts. This review only confirmed our faith in the judgment surrounding them. The cyclical result proved insensitive even to large changes in the estimating parameters used to set cost on the aqueducts; were the factors to be halved, the peaks would still be sharply evident.

ANALYSIS AND EVALUATION OF RESULTING CYCLES

The construction cycle, isolated above, is meaningful only when it is placed in its own organizational and manpower environment. Accordingly, in the following chapter we discuss: (1) the administrative procedures by which construction was performed in the period, (2) the labor management system, and (3) problems created by uneven construction cycles. In Chapter 4 and 7 we evaluate the emperors' separate performances as planners and as managers.

ENDNOTES TO CHAPTER II

[1]This research by the authors was reported originally in an article, "Manpower Needs for the Public Works Programs of the Julio-Claudian Emperors," *Journal of Economic History* XLIII, No. 2 (June, 1983), 373–378, here revised and used with permission.

[2]S. B. Platner and T. Ashby, *A Topographical Dictionary of Ancient Rome* (London, 1929), cited as *PA*. To this we added Frank C. Bourne, *Public Works of the Julio-Claudians and the Flavians* (Princeton, N.J., 1941) and Ernest Nash, *Pictorial Dictionary of Ancient Rome*, 2 vols. (New York, 1968, 2nd edition). These were supplemented by Rodolfo Lanciani, *The Ruins and Excavations of Ancient Rome* (New York, 1897-reissued 1967), J. H. Middleton, *The Remains of Ancient Rome*, 2 vols. (London and Edinburgh, 1892), and any new archaeological evidence available. Some constructions, such as the aqueducts, required greater detail. The most essential work for aqueduct study is an ancient source, Frontinus, *Aq.*, supplemented by T. Ashby, *The Aqueducts of Ancient Rome* and Esther Van Deman, *The Building of the Roman Aqueducts* (Washington, D.C., 1934). Occasionally, for more details on a specific building, we used other sources.

[3]*The Economy of the Roman Empire* (Cambridge, 1974), 90–114; 157–223.

[4]*A History of Architecture* (revised by J. C. Palmes), (New York, 1975), 276.

[5]*Princeton Encyclopedia of Classical Sites* (Princeton, N.J., 1976), 616.

[6]Cf. with *ILS* 6086, 28 where the same index of building size is used.

[7]Marion E. Blake, *Ancient Roman Construction in Italy from Prehistoric Periods to Augustus* (Washington, 1947), 178–179.

[8]Middleton, II, 210.

[9]Nash, II, 291.

[10]Blake, 132.

[11]Joseph A. Schumpeter, *Business Cycles* (New York, 1939), I, 170.

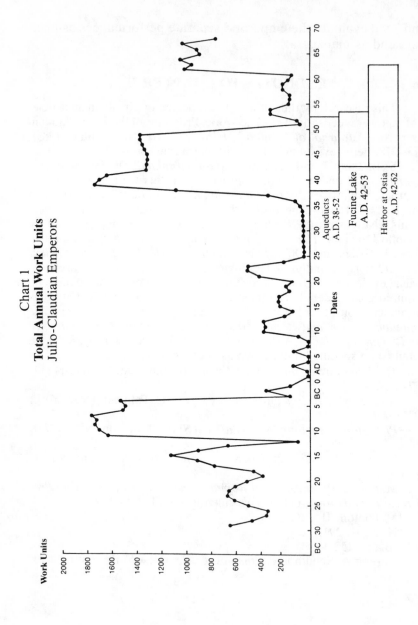

Chart 1
Total Annual Work Units
Julio-Claudian Emperors

Chart 1. Total Work Units. Julio-Claudian Emperors

Data Sheet for Chart 1

Augustus

29	BC	643	2	BC	354	25	44	50	719

Augustus					Tiberius etc.			Caligula etc.		Nero etc.	

29 BC	643	2 BC	354	25	44	50	719
28	462	1 BC	156	26	44	51	73
27	353	1 AD	10	27	44	52	104
26	339	2	25	28	54	53	314
25	546	3	146	29	44	54	314
24	613	4	10	30	44		
23	673	5	10	31	44	**Nero**	
22	663	6	123	32	44		
21	641	7	15	33	44	55	170
20	470	8	10	34	48	56	160
19	378	9	106	35	77	57	160
18	458	10	376	36	97	58	210
17	764	11	358	37	347	59	221
16	908	12	371			60	175
15	1122	13	208	**Caligula**		61	140
14	916	14	135			62	1015
13	666			38	1073	63	950
12	63	**Tiberius**		39	1760	64	1040
11	1631			40	1695	65	882
10	1710	15	239	41	1635	66	865
9	1738	16	244			67	1018
8	1726	17	215	**Claudius**		68	755
7	1770	18	160				
6	1520	19	185	42	1310		
5	1496	20	135	43	1315		
4	1531	21	403	44	1310		
3	160	22	513	45	1310		
		23	508	46	1330		
		24	204	47	1349		
				48	1363		
				49	1363		

Aqua Claudia and Anio Novus on Porta Praenestina

III. ADMINISTRATION OF PUBLIC WORKS AND LABOR MANAGEMENT

During the Republic, the officials responsible both for the maintenance of existing public works and for the initiation of new building programs were the censors. Since the recordings of the censorial activities are inconsistent, it is difficult to understand exactly how the system worked. We do know that censors were normally appointed once every five years but actually served for a term of only 18 months. Thus, there was no one in day-to-day supervision of the public works program. To allocate the work, the censors normally let maintenance contracts by public bidding for the entire five year period and let new construction projects on a "job" basis. The Senate determined in advance the funds available for each five year period. We are not certain whether the funds were in two separate votes or were lumped into one pot; thus, we do not know whether the censors had discretion in allocating the total between maintenance and new construction. For major projects, working capital was provided by paying the contractor half the final price in advance.[1] Quality control was addressed by the censor's review of previous work done by the contractor before giving the same contractor a new contract.[2] Theoretically, the censors made the decisions as to what new construction would be performed; however, there were several instances in which their plans were challenged by the Senate, sometimes successfully, sometimes not.[3] We can be certain that the Senate, during discussion of the initial allocation of funds, would have made a careful evaluation of the larger needs of the city so that for major projects an understanding would have been reached with the newly appointed censors as to which ones would be undertaken. The first recorded formal, long-range, broad-gauge plan for the growth of the city seems to have been prepared around 179 B.C. during Cato's censorship. This plan included many different forms of public utility and transportation systems plus basic plans for the future of the Forum.[4]

Because of the shortness of a censor's term of office, it was impossible to have a continuous, coherent public works policy;[5]

31

on the other hand, the Senate was reluctant to lengthen officially the censor's normal term (Livy, 45.15). Consequently, no one successfully tried to modernize the system for managing public works until the time of Sulla. In 82 B.C. the dictator, rich with the spoils of his campaigns and with the permission of the Senate to rebuild the Temple of Capitoline Jupiter, carried out public works requiring a lengthy period of time. As Strong noted, "The Sullan episode, although it did not produce a consistent programme of prestige public building, paved the way for a new conception of public building as an instrument of power in the struggle for supremacy at the end of the Republic."[6] Like Sulla, Caesar recognized the value of public building as propaganda: he, too, began to develop a public works program.

Even the aediles, who were not normally considered a part of the construction-monitoring system, saw the propaganda and political advancement opportunities of the public works programs; therefore, under their general *cura urbis* duties (normally maintenance tasks) they spent large sums of money on buildings connected with public entertainment, a valuable asset on a man's record early in his career.[7] Since there was always an aedile in office, Augustus later used this position to provide continuity to all building programs (see below).

We need to mention one alternate means of funding certain of the construction and maintenance needs of the city. It had become a tradition for prominent citizens to assume responsibility from their own private funds for the construction, maintenance, or both, of certain clearly public buildings. Usually citizens paid for these buildings from the *manubiae* resulting from their successful military campaigns. Thus, their name would be associated with (not-to-be-forgotten) victories. An example of a major, clearly public, building whose maintenance had been accepted as a private, hereditary family duty, was the Basilica Aemilia. Its maintenance was so accepted by the Aemilian family (Cicero, *Pro Sestio*, 116; *Pro Plancio*, 78). Similarly, Gaius Octavius built the first porticus as a victory monument in 168 B.C. (*RG* 4.3).

Augustus used the tradition of private payment for the costs of public buildings as a way to gain personal credit for much of the construction work which he later accomplished as Emperor; by that time the distinction between the private fortune of the Emperor and the public funds of the realm had started to blur. For example, in his *Res Gestae* he says:

> Four times I aided the public treasury with my own money, paying out in this manner to those in charge of the treasury one hundred and fifty million sesterces. . . . On my own ground I built the Temple of Mars Ultor and the Augustan Forum from the spoils of war (ch. 17 & ch. 21).[8]

Some time before Augustus started his reforms of the public works management system, it had become obvious that the management system required an overhaul. Sulla's work was essentially intended to get needed construction work done but he did not do much with the structure of the process of management. His efforts to secure central supervision of a project until it was completed, regardless of the expiry of the censor's mandate, were limited to a subterfuge: he appointed curators to manage each segment of the program. Curators were officials of lower rank whose term of office did not expire until the work was done. This use of curators as monitors had originated in the previous century, perhaps during the term of L. Metellus as censor (*CIL* 6.3824).

Caesar took advantage of another weakness of the existing system: the lack of long-range utilitarian-based planning. In the words of Strong: "It is clear that Caesar was taking over the complete control of the building policy, setting up his own staff of architects and advisors and aiming at the complete transformation of the city.[9] Some of Caesar's work was completed; his death halted further progress.

It was for Augustus to complete and to expand on the dreams of Caesar. Using the traditional tendency of the aediles to move into an arena technically that of the censors, Augustus, always shy of seeming to break precedent, appointed Agrippa aedile, a title well below that appropriate to Augustus' factotum. Agrippa expanded the title into a major innovation in the field of public works management. Not only did he complete an impressive sequence of major projects, using Augustus' "personal funds" rather than Senate controlled ones,[10] but he created a permanent body, the Water Board (Front. *Aq.* 2.98), under the control of the Emperor to plan for, to carry out, and to manage this essential aspect of Rome's imperial progress. In managing to get public works constructed by means of an unprestigious position (aedile) and, more importantly, by paying for the construction with his own personal funds, Augustus, breaking no precedent and theoretically leaving the Senate in charge, made the public works program the prerogative of the Emperor. Augustus, however, still maintained that work was done *ex auctoritate senatus*. It was left for Claudius to change the meaningless phrase to *ex auctoritate Caesaris* (*CIL* 6.3154–5). Strong sums it up: "The Augustan system, introduced with a minimum of change, but curing some of the most serious weaknesses of the Republican system, remained the basis of the public work administration throughout the Empire."[11]

Labor Management

The Romans used two separate systems to administer their public works programs during the Julio-Claudian period:

Imperial civil servants, the *familia Caesaris*, usually slaves, the property of the Emperor, performed routine work. This work force handled minor emergencies, small repair projects, and preventive maintenance. It was kept routinely busy, undoubtedly using the kind of work allocation and priority system used throughout the world, that is, "immediate work" when needed and "programmable work" to fill in the low spots in the immediate work demands. Larger projects were done by contract.[12]

Contractors performed new construction, major rebuilding, and reconstruction work. They were used to handle major bulges in the workloads. Contractors then had to keep their own force busy through successful bidding on construction projects, whether in the public or in the private sector.

We have already stated that the Imperial civil servants were usually slaves. However, a contractor might possibly use primarily slave labor, primarily free or freedman labor, or any mixture of the two. It is possible that the problems of managing the city's work force would be different depending on the kind of labor that was involved. Thus, we need to discuss at some length the nature of the slave system in the construction trades in Rome at the time.

According to A. H. M. Jones, before the establishment of the Principate, the primary sources for slaves were the wars of Augustus in Spain, Germany, the Alpine areas, and Illyricum and Pannonia. After Augustus had consolidated his power, the establishment of law and order eliminated piracy and brigandage, the other main sources. From then on, most slaves seem to have been bred.[13] If we are to assume, as seems justified, that most slaves used in Rome during the period were bred, then we can also assume that their careers were made for them by their masters; that is, a master secured a boy or an untrained slave and carefully trained him to an occupation of the master's choosing.[14] Further, we can assume that the master could afford to be careful in the slave's training; expenditures on a good apprenticeship would be the equivalent of sharpening a tool. Because the slave was the absolute property of his master, an investment in the slave could not be lost, as it would be in the case of a free man, through the man's leaving for better opportunities if he turned out to be very able. As for a freeborn, the probability of his getting a carefully planned and financed apprenticeship depended on his parents or on his pulling himself up by his own bootstraps. Since we are talking about artisan labor, it is unlikely that a freeborn laborer would have parents who could finance an apprenticeship. It is a fully supportable hypothesis that slave artisans were the elite of their professions. In the words of William L. Westermann, "slaves continued to be bought as investment, trained in a particular *techne,* and leased or sold as income-producing property."[15]

Industry practice supports this hypothesis. As Brunt says: "It would have been wasteful to maintain slaves for industrial or commercial operations that did not provide continuous employment. Thus though building contractors had permanent gangs of slaves, these gangs (like those under the curators of the aqueducts) would not have sufficed in times of a building boom, such as . . . the commencement of any large programme of public works. It must be remembered that public building was not continuous."[16] The continuously employed experienced labor was slave; the casually employed was free. We can suspect that in the practical environment of a work situation the free worked for a slave foreman. In times of low demand for labor, the free man would be let go (*CIL* III, 948). The free man would be used if it was dangerous; who wants to risk a valuable piece of property? (Varro, *RR* 1.17).

We can summarize: The core workforce was slave; the casual workforce was usually free. In times of modest unemployment, the burden would have fallen on the free men; in times of severe unemployment, the burden would have fallen on the foreman and on the contractor, the owner of the slave cadre. As Bloch states for nondomestic servants: "At all times one [a slave's owner] was forced to find a remunerative outlet for it [slave labor] in production for the market."[17] If no market was found, the owner still needed to maintain his slaves; pressures to find work for them would have been intense. The contractor had bought his slaves for a price. While he might sell them, he would not starve them during adversity any more than a farmer would starve his horses in winter. As Brunt notes: "the freeman might go in want, but self-interest and, later, imperial rescripts (*Coll.* 3.3) required the master to support his slave and treat him well."[18] The slave always had the protection of his master to this extent— since the slave was a piece of property belonging to his master, anyone harming him attacked the rights of the owner.[19]

The institution of slavery has only a little bearing on the problem of unemployment. In Rome the person hurt by the un-availability of jobs was never the slave; the one hurt was either a contractor or the free laborer. If there is no work for a slave, the owner is usually the one who is hurt. In a similar situation a free laborer carries the burden of unemployment himself. If his income is insufficient to support a family, his only recourse is the dole. Yet in the words of Brunt: "The number of recipients of the dole was artificially limited, hence many free inhabitants of Rome had to buy all their own food. . . . And even the *plebs frumentaria* needed cash. The grain ration of five modii a month was more than enough for a single man (though the *pistores* to whom it must have been taken for milling and baking presumably retained part of it) but insufficient for a family. . . ."[20] As Donald Sippel notes: "Life for the Roman poor was an endless crisis. The difficulty of securing adequate housing, of meeting the often exorbitant rent demanded by speculator-landlords, of finding employment, even of the sort requiring nothing beyond a strong back were all problems of the disadvantaged of Rome."[21] No emperor could afford to be indifferent to the needs of the common people; riots were the weapons of the citizens. Without employment there was little else they could do except sell themselves back into slavery; there were a significant number of cases where freedmen did just that.[22]

Problems from Irregular Manpower Demand

Sharp changes in the demand for labor within any society—even primitive ones—cause important social and economic problems. Workmen must come from somewhere or be transferred from alternate employment. In the Roman case, labor apparently came to Rome before 29 B.C. from two sources: first, the slave population in the city was enlarged by the influx of war captives from the military campaigns of the Late Republic.[23] Second, free agricultural labor was displaced by slaves. This labor source, although hard to document, can be seen in the significant movements from the land to the city of Rome.[24]

On the other side of the cycle, sharp reductions in construction work could present serious manpower problems. Within our time period, sharp reductions took place after 7 B.C. and after A.D. 51. These periods of cutback in government contracts required simultaneous developments in other portions of the society to explain what happened to the displaced labor. We have stated earlier that private contractors performed major construction and major repair. They could not easily ignore their redundant workers. A public purse might have been willing to clothe and to feed idled public employees; private contractors surely would not have been able to feed idle workers. We can postulate at least four developments. First, the redundant workers might have left the city for the countryside. Second, the workers might have been reemployed on different assignments—as soldiers, or as clean up crews after fires, pestilences or floods. Third, private building might have taken up when public construction ceased. Fourth, they might have remained in Rome, unemployed and underfed, subsisting on scraps, odd jobs, and a patron's unwilling largesse. A fifth development, the harbor of Ostia, suggests that the post-A.D. 50 downturn really did not exist. The first two of these developments are unlikely to have been much help; the last three are credible hypotheses.

An Exodus From Rome

There is no evidence of a well-timed exodus of unemployed construction workers from Rome. To the extent that they were slaves, they would have no home to welcome them back; they had not come to Rome from Italian farms to which they could return. Further, historical evidence from many places suggests that labor rarely if ever leaves a city once it has been attracted to it.[25] A hypothesis requiring a mass movement of unemployed to the countryside is simply unacceptable. However, it is possible that a reduction in numbers through natural causes did alleviate the problem during the low point in construction. Most authorities believe that without inputs from external sources, the city's population would have declined.[26] If the city ceased to attract new residents, we can suggest that her population would have declined over the period of low labor demand. The Early Empire inter-peak period was 38 years long; natural population losses would perhaps have reduced labor redundancy significantly during so long a period.

Reassignment to Emergency Clean-ups

There are other developments (fires, floods, wars, etc.) which might have provided employment for men released from their completed public construction jobs. We have not explored these possibilities in any depth. There were major fires in at least 10 B.C., A.D. 22, A.D. 27, A.D. 36 and certainly A.D. 64. There were plagues in 23 B.C., A.D. 6, and A.D. 65. There were, however, no important wars during the period; the capital, further, was not usually a source for conscription of soldiers.

Generally speaking, the unpredictability of such events does not make them good unemployment cures. Natural disasters occur as frequently during labor shortages as in times of redundancy.

Private Building

The hypothesis that private building took over where public building left off is a more attractive one. If we presume that public building is the engine that drives the private economy, we can suggest that labor was attracted into (or directed into) the city for public construction work. As a result of the increased labor force there existed severe housing shortages, which then, as a secondary boom, fueled a private housing boom to follow on and employ building labor freed as the original source of employment disappeared.

Such a hypothesis fits very nicely into the 20th century theories of Joseph Schumpeter. According to those theories a major "innovation"—either technical, social, or political—generates a sharp, hard boost to a society. The innovation then generates secondary and tertiary employment, slowly dying down as the original investment and its reverberations pass into history.[27] In the case at hand, the major political events surrounding the transfer from Republic to Principate and from Italian power to a Mediterranean power would become Schumpeter's "innovation." Such a scenario would predict a true depression about— in our time frame—A.D. 25 in the reign of Tiberius.

Tenney Frank suggests, however, that the "Augustan Prosperity" was congruent with Augustus' building programs rather than a follow-on to them.[28] If this is true then private building would have been cycle-enhancing rather than cycle-reducing. The labor problems would have been magnified when both private and public building slowed down at the same time.

Conceptually, it is obvious that private building would follow very closely on public buildings. Workmen were in the city: they had to eat, to sleep, and to keep from freezing. Indeed, aqueducts, the biggest item in the program, were probably already needed to service a population suffering from lack of support.

Persistent Under-Employment

Possibly the unemployed from the completed public building programs looking for ways to support themselves went into a vast variety of small entrepreneurial businesses, probably not profitable but capable of aiding in the minimum support of otherwise underemployed labor. Hopkins speaks of "a fantastic fragmentation of services and retail sales" in contemporary underdeveloped capitals.[29] Roman men of property had become very wealthy by the time of the Principate. Petronius in his *Satyricon* also portrays a range of hangers-on and parasites who, without employment, subsisted on the leavings from rich men's tables. One development might be a persistent and long continuing trend toward a parasite class, underemployed and nonproductive, but provided support through private relief.

Next, we will discuss how individual emperors handled their labor forces and their problems. We hope to determine whether they managed them in accordance with a plan or they left them to solve themselves haphazardly.

ENDNOTES TO CHAPTER III

[1]Cf. the Puteoli Inscription, *CIL* 1.215.6.

[2]P. A. Brunt, "Free Labour," *JRS* 70 (1980), 85.

[3]Vell. 1.15.3; Cf. Appian, *BC* 1.28.125.

[4]D. E. Strong, "The Administration of Public Building in Rome during the Late Republic and Early Empire," *Institute of Classical Studies Bulletin* 15 (1968), 97.

[5]T. Mommsen, *Römisches Staatsrecht*, 3rd ed. (Leipzig, 1887), II, 449.

[6]Strong, 101. See also Paul MacKendrick, *The Mute Stones Speak* (New York, 1960), 117.

[7]Strong, 99.

[8]Trans. by F. W. Shipley, *Res Gestae Divi Augusti*, Loeb Classical Library (1961), 373; 379.

[9]Strong, 102.

[10]For more about Agrippa's work, see F. W. Shipley, *Agrippa's Building Activities at Rome* (St. Louis, 1933); and H. B. Evans, "Agrippa's Water Plan," *AJA* 86 (1982), 401–16; J. Roddaz, *Marcus Agrippa* (Rome, 1984), 252–91.

[11]Strong, 104.

[12]P. A. Brunt, "Free Labour and Public Works at Rome," *JRS* 70 (1980), 85.

[13]"Slavery in the Ancient World," *The Economic History Review,* 2nd ser., 9 (1956), 193. This article is included in *Slavery in Classical Antiquity,* ed. by M. I. Finley (Cambridge, 1959), 193.1–15.

[14]Susan Treggiari, *Roman Freedmen During the Late Republic* (Oxford, 1969), 85.

[15]*The Slave Systems of Greek and Roman Antiquity* (Philadelphia, 1955), 98.

[16]"Free Labor," 93.

[17]Marc Bloch, *Slavery and Serfdom in the Middle Ages* (Berkeley, 1975), 4.

[18]Review of W. L. Westermann, "The Slave System," *JRS* 48 (1958), 167. For improvement in slave conditions, see Westermann, 114–115.

[19]Thomas Wiedemann, *Greek and Roman Slavery* (Baltimore, Md. and London, 1981), 10. There is some evidence for the theory that the Roman emperors did try to improve the lot of slaves. This evidence is based on Suet. *Claudius* 25 and Dio Cassius, 60 (61), 29. Wiedemann does not believe that the Romans nor the emperors had a humane attitude towards the slaves (p. 184).

[20]"Free Labour and Public Works at Rome," *JRS* 70 (1980), 94.

[21]Donald V. Sippel, "Dietary Deficiency Among the Lower Classes of Late Republican and Early Imperial Rome," *AncW* 16 (1987), 49.

[22]Brunt, "Review," 167–168. For more discussion, see Alexander Szakats, "Slavery as a Social and Economic Institution in Antiquity," *Prudentia* V.7.1 (1975), 37–38, W. L. Westermann, *The Slave Systems of Greek and Roman Antiquity* (Philadelphia, 1955), 59, and Susan Treggiari, *Roman Freedmen,* 2.

[23]Keith Hopkins, *Conquerors and Slaves* (Cambridge, 1978), 102; P. A. Brunt, *Italian Manpower* (London, 1971), 119.

[24]Caes. *BG* 2.23; Cic. *Ad Att.* 5.205; Livy, 45.34. For other details see A. M. Duff, *Freedman in the Early Roman Empire* (Oxford, 1928), 2 and Treggiari, *Roman Freedmen,* 1.

[25]Examples are common in recent developmental theory, where efforts to evaluate the magnet effects of a central city are common. See Bruce London, "Is the Primate City Parasitic" in *Journal of Developing Areas,* 12 (October, 1977), 49; Alajandro Portes and Harley L. Browning, eds., *Current Perspectives in Latin-American Urban Research* (Austin, 1976); Nigel Harris, *Economic Development, Cities and Planning: The Case of Bombay* (Bombay, 1978).

[26]Brunt, *Ital. Man.,* 338.

[27]Schumpeter, I, 97 ff.

[28]*ESAR,* V. 19.

[29]Hopkins, 107, n. 19.

IV. EARLIER JULIO-CLAUDIAN EMPERORS

Our objective in evaluating the performance of the individual emperors as managers is to correlate the peaks and the valleys in the building cycle with policy shifts either initiated from the managerial style of each emperor or, alternatively, forced by external events. We will take them in chronological order, starting with Augustus.

THE AUGUSTAN APPROACH

As a man possessing newly acquired *imperium,* Augustus had, above all, two immediate tasks: first, to catch up with nearly 15 years of neglected maintenance, an inevitable result of the Civil War, and second, to create a set of visible monuments to his position. His performance at these two tasks created the first irregularity in the building cycle: the mini-boom of 27–12 B.C. We cut off the mini-boom at 12 B.C. because at that time Augustus' programs suddenly blossomed into a major water-supply-based peak. The mini-boom was composed of a mass of small projects and a few large ones. He boasted in his *Res Gestae* (19 and the summary 2–3) of repairing 82 temples. None of these had much impact on his workload, but they would have established him as a believer in the old values and in the customs of the *mos maiorum,* essential to the creation of his desired image.

With one exception, Augustus obviously planned his major works during the mini-boom to cater to the popular taste, to settle him into his role as a "friend of the people." The exception was his other major project, the Aqua Virgo, a fulfillment of a major need, for water. The major "friend-of-the-people" projects consisted of a bath (Thermae Agrippae, 25–21 B.C.) and two theaters (of Marcellus, 17–13 B.C. and of Balbus, 13–12 B.C.).

We can conclude that Augustus' mini-boom programs, unlike his later ones, were essentially public relations efforts, needed to build an image for the dynasty and to confirm him personally in power.

The macro-boom which followed Augustus' mini-boom was primarily a water supply one, with the reconstruction of all of

Theater of Marcellus

Rome's aqueducts plus the creation of the Aqua Alsietina. Nevertheless, several administrative or recreational projects were also included. Unlike the water projects, there was flexibility available for these projects; their pattern shows a neat sense of timing. Notice how the projects dovetail into each other to create a relatively smooth workload:

Constructions	Dates	Work Units
Saepta	29–26 B.C.	594
Thermae	25–19 B.C.	1125
Theater (Marcellus)	18–13 B.C.	2208
Theater (Balbus)	13–12 B.C.	1790
Cohortes Vigilium	10– 8 B.C.	754
Diribitorium	10– 7 B.C.	394
Forum of Augustus	2 B.C.	580

From the data above, one can tentatively conclude that Augustus was coordinating his manpower availability with his project schedule; a central plan seems to have been in operation. Thus, upon finishing one project he immediately began a new one. For example, after the completion of his Thermae in 19 B.C., he started the construction of his Theater of Marcellus in 18 B.C. Upon its completion, he began to build the Theater of Balbus. During this period the emperor employed his labor force rationally.

Although in constructing his administrative and his recreational buildings, Augustus managed his labor well. In constructing his last major group of constructions, the aqueducts, the emperor used his labor for a longer continuous time and in greater numbers. The aqueduct constructions (with their dates and work units) were as follows:

Constructions	Dates	Work Units
Aqua Virgo	24–19 B.C.	2295
Restorations	11– 4 B.C.	8487
Aqua Alsietina	11– 4 B.C.	3281

These constructions were the predominant contributors to the striking peak which occurred between 11 B.C. and 4 B.C. There are, however, possible explanations that might account for the peak and might reduce its labor management impact. First, perhaps Augustus used his permanent maintenance force to do significant portions of the work. Second, in constructing an aqueduct both the type of work required and, thus, the type of labor force needed is not always the same: in the outlying districts aqueduct building consists, primarily, of tunneling and of cutting and filling; near the city it consists, mainly, of arch making since here the aqueducts run on arches. In the outlying districts the labor force might be an agricultural one; near the city it would undoubtedly be skilled in urban building work. The outlying aqueduct labor force might be quite distant from Rome; the Anio Vetus stretches 38 miles from the city; the Aqua Marcia, 45 miles. The managers might have renovated the farther ends of these aqueducts with local rather than with city labor; thus, they limited the variability of city labor demand.

Finally, five of the seven aqueducts in Augustan constructions were restorations rather than new constructions. It is extremely difficult to determine the exact amount of repair or of reconstruction that Augustus actually did on these renovations. The emperor inflates his accomplishments in *Res Gestae;* his restorations, therefore, may have averaged no more than heavy routine repair work. The original manpower study allowed 40% of the original cost as Augustus' cost of restoration. This could be too high. If 20% had been used instead as the cost, the peak would have been reduced.

From the beginning of his reign, Augustus' use of manpower rose steadily upward with relative smoothness. In about 2 B.C., however, something happened: the emperor suddenly stopped building. At the time he was 61 years old and had been in power for 25 years. What happened? What caused his indifference? Was he merely bored with the job? Was he ill? Had he lost interest in his would-be successor? Did he run out of work? Did he run out of money? One plausible explanation is worth mentioning. From his ascent to power, Augustus was fortunate in having as his chief executive Agrippa, an outstanding manager.[1] Thus, it is possible that Augustus had depended on Agrippa to plan his work; when Agrippa's plans had been carried out, no one had the foresight and the imagination to carry on Agrippa's planning and managing job for Augustus.

In summary, Augustus up until around 2 B.C. had a firm control on his labor force and on his work projects. After finishing one project he would then start on another, thereby showing a carefully thought-out coordination of projects with the available labor force.

Mausoleum of Augustus

THE TIBERIAN TROUGH

Augustus' strong and rational management of his building program came abruptly to an end in 4 B.C. Although there were still fifteen years left in Augustus' reign, we will try to pin this collapse on Tiberius and in the process transfer a bit of the credit for earlier outstanding work load management from Augustus to his able lieutenant Agrippa. A review of the underlying data makes it clear that the construction of the Aqua Alsietina and the restoration of all the older aqueducts sustained the late stages of the Augustan boom. With their completion the work load collapsed from 1500 work units in 4 B.C. to about 200 work units in 3 B.C. Marcus Agrippa, Augustus' right hand man, planned the preliminary directions for these projects as his last efforts before he died in 12 B.C. To complete them required the next eight years.[2] The succeeding trough lasts for the remainder of Augustus' reign (to A.D. 14) and for all of Tiberius' (to A.D. 37). Since on Agrippa's death Tiberius inherited the planning and the work management role which Agrippa had formerly performed for Augustus, an hypothesis that Tiberius was the sole instigator of the Tiberian Trough is tempting. Thus, Tiberius can possibly be the "new face in the picture" who was primarily responsible for all the thin building programs of the entire period (4 B.C.-A.D. 37). Although this hypothesis is plausible, we cannot consider it until we have explored two alternate explanations for the policy change. One of these is that the regime ran out of work to do; the other that it ran out of money.

How probable is it that, when Tiberius was in charge of the building program, there was no need to do any constructions? We stated earlier that the Julio-Claudian emperors on achieving the imperium had three primary public works objectives for the imperial city: for food, for drink, for entertainment. We can see from Appendix 2 that Augustus had progressed: For drink, he had just restored all the older aqueducts (11–4 B.C.) and had completed two new ones, the Aqua Virgo (19 B.C.) and the Aqua Alsietina (4 B.C.). For entertainment, he had constructed a major bath (25–19 B.C.) and had completed two theaters (those of Marcellus and of Balbus) in 13 B.C. Consequently, the government had taken care of two of its primary concerns, the water supply and the entertainment of the populace. But was the food supply adequate? Earlier Julius Caesar had worried about Rome's food supply: he had proposed a canal to provide a protected waterway for the food ships; he suggested building a harbor at Ostia (Plut. *Caes*. 58.10) to insure them a safe harbor. In addition, he had planned to drain the Pomptine marshes and the Fucine Lake to provide productive land for thousands of men (Suet. *Caes*. 45 and Plut. *Caes*. 58.10). As Meiggs says "Augustus was by temperament more cautious and, unlike Caesar, he determined to build the new order securely before tackling public works that could wait. His large-scale building in Rome was essential to his social policy; for his corn supply he was content to provide the basis of a more effective administration."[3] Carcopino, however, sees it differently. "If one believes the scholiast of Horace, he [Augustus] started the enterprise [the harbor of Ostia]; but at the death of Agrippa, he suspended the enterprise."[4] It stretches the imagination that Tiberius did not consider famine a major problem. We have said earlier that Augustus charged Tiberius with solving a serious food shortage early in the Principate. When Tiberius failed in this mission, he had to be bailed out by Augustus himself (Suet. *Tib*. 8). We also know that there was a serious wheat shortage in A.D. 5 (Dio 55.26, 1–3) and in A.D. 6 (Dio 55.26.1; 27.1 ff; Pliny, *NH* 7.129), and again in A.D. 19 (Tac. *Ann*. 2.87; Suet. *Tib*. 48).[5] There can be no question that both Tiberius and Augustus were fully aware of the need for major construction to solve recurrent food crises.

We cannot accept the hypothesis that the Tiberian Trough resulted from the exhaustion of the need for new construction; until the food supply had been assured, there was an obvious and expensive demand for public works to protect Rome from famine. We must seek the reason for the Tiberian Trough elsewhere.

The second hypothesis for the cause of the trough is that the government simply ran out of money or that new projects could not be initiated because Augustus' extensive building programs had depleted available financial resources.

We do have a set of figures which shed some light on the financial position of the period:

First, we do know that Tiberius in A.D. 14 inherited from Augustus 100,000,000 sesterces in the emperor's privy purse, the fiscus (Suet. *Aug*. 101.2).

Second, Tiberius in A.D. 37 left to Caligula 2,700,000,000 sesterces in the fiscus (Suet. *Calig*. 37.3).

Third, if we assume that the total amount of money that Tiberius had available to him at the end of his reign was the

2,700,000,000 sesterces which he left to Caligula (Suet. *Calig*. 37.3) and if we subtract the starting figure of 100,000,000 sesterces from that ending figure, we get 2,600,000,000 sesterces gain during his reign. If we then divide the total by 23 (the number of years in Tiberius' reign), we can calculate from these data that on the average Tiberius ran a surplus in his treasury of over 110,000,000 sesterces per year throughout his reign. Rodewald (p. 11) suggests that the figures for the starting amount are for the fiscus only while the ending figures may be for both the fiscus and the aerarium; thus the two figures are not compatible.[6] If Rodewald's hypothesis is correct, the starting figure might have been larger, the average gain per year smaller. In this case, Tiberius was not as poor as Frank (see below) believed him to be at the start of his reign. Since our objective in this analysis is to determine whether Tiberius was too poor to build, Rodewald's alternate hypothesis on the beginning figure further supports our belief that Tiberius was *not* too poor to build.

Fourth, as a reference point, Pliny tells us that the Aqua Claudia, begun in A.D. 37, right after Tiberius' reign, cost 350,000,000 sesterces (*NH* 36.122). Thus, if Rodewald's worries are ignored, Tiberius could have financed a major aqueduct in a little over 3 years simply by balancing his budget.

We have treated the above data cautiously, particularly in view of the length of the period. Thus, when Tiberius assumed the Principate he had, according to Tenney Frank's estimate, annual revenue (gross of expenditures) of 500,000,000 sesterces. The emperor could see only enough in the fiscus to finance three months' worth of expenditures.[7] For a newly made emperor, this is not enough to provide much assurance. Worse, it is possible that his knowledge of incoming revenues was uncertain. He was by nature a cautious man. In addition, we do not know the rate of flow either of income or of expenditures; it is possible that early in the reign accretions of reserves proceeded at a much slower pace. Tiberius' forecasts of revenue may have been far more pessimistic than we can realize from hindsight.

Nevertheless, the uncertainty should not have lasted for long. The accretions of reserves are too large to have all been achieved in the last half of his reign. By approximately A.D. 25 Tiberius should have realized that he had enough money to meet the obvious needs of his citizens. At least by A.D. 33 we can be absolutely certain that he was running enormous surpluses; the financial crisis of that year, given the enormity of the Tiberian building trough, is a classic textbook example of a govermentally caused crisis resulting from a huge government surplus.

With Tiberius locking so much of the empire's money in his treasury, the Roman public suffered from a shortage of money in circulation. Tacitus (*Ann.* 6.17) describes the panic:

> Hence followed a scarcity of money, a great shock being given to all credit, the current coin too, in consequence of the conviction of so many persons and the sale of their property, being locked up in the imperial treasury or the public exchequer. To meet this, the Senate had directed that every creditor should have two-thirds of his capital secured on estates in Italy. Creditors however were suing for payment in full, and it was not respectable for persons when sued to break faith. So, at first, there were clamorous meetings and importunate entreaties; then noisy applications to the praetor's court. And the very device intended as a remedy, the sale and purchase of estates, proved the contrary, as the usurers had hoarded up all their money for buying land. The facilities for selling were followed by a fall of prices, and the deeper a man was in debt, the more reluctantly did he part with his property, and many were utterly ruined. The destruction of private wealth precipitated the fall of rank and reputation, till at last the emperor interposed his aid by distributing throughout the banks a hundred million sesterces, and allowing freedom to borrow without interest for three years, provided the borrower gave security to the State in land to double the amount.[8]

Secondary sources do not always agree with the above analysis; some of them indeed suggest that Tiberius was short of money. Levick, for example, basing her analysis on Suetonius, says ". . . the shortage of bullion led Tiberius to take an interest in other men's money and property even to the point of having charges brought against them so that he might confiscate their wealth or its source (mines) . . ."[9] The ancient author Suetonius does not mention the "shortage of bullion" as the reason for Tiberius' money-grabbing (Suet. *Tib.* 49). Tenney Frank, likewise, suggests that "Perhaps the decrease in coinage mentioned above had actually been due to the exhaustion of the bullion then obtainable by the treasury. We may also be justified in surmising that the heavier minting of gold and silver by Caligula was made possible by Tiberius' expropriation of mines."[10] Rodewald has done an excellent job of demolishing both Levick's and Frank's suggestions.[11] The development of Tiberius' enormous surplus of spare cash by his death only four years after the crisis makes it hard to accept any explanation for Tiberius' rapacity except unadorned commitment to penury and to miserliness. Pliny's worry (*NH* 6.101; 12.84) about the loss of exchange to the Far East is probably but a minor issue. (How could Pliny know its value?) In actuality almost all of the cash disappeared into Tiberius' fiscus, not to reappear until after his death.

The numismatists have paid some attention to the sharp reduction in the minting of new coins between 10 B.C. and the end of Tiberius' reign, perhaps leaving the impression that this was a cause of the shortage of money.[12] This is an unlikely cause and effect relationship; the minting of new coins is inappropriate when a government runs a surplus. Using modern sources, Hopkins has estimated that the loss or the destruction rate for small coins should be in the order of 2 percent per year.[13] At that rate, the government would be required to issue new coins only if the money supply went down more sharply (2%) than did the rate of economic activity. We have no direct measure of economic activity, and are unlikely to see an acceptable one developed. We can perhaps estimate *increased* economic activity if it is continued over a reasonable period, that is, long enough to be certain that all the possible unused coins in the treasury have been issued, but the reduction in coinage cannot go below zero: thus, any economic recession which is greater than the coinage loss and destruction rate will show no new minting, except for those minted for public relations or for political reasons.

To summarize the evidence, we cannot accept a hypothesis that the treasury of Tiberius was so depleted as to prevent the initiation of new construction except, perhaps, for a few years at the beginning of his reign. After that time, the only defensible hypothesis is that the emperor was collecting cash in his fiscus, rather than suffering for lack of it. At the time of his death, there is no doubt: he was awash with cash, two billion seven hundred million sesterces of it.

We have dealt with the only two reasons why the Tiberian Trough might have occurred because of circumstances beyond the control of the emperor. We are left with the belief that the trough was the intentional, thought-out decision of an individual who believed, perhaps for doctrinaire reasons, in a strongly conservative and austere regimen, one who would allow the best interests of his people to be subordinated to a Stoic philosophy.[14]

Conclusion

The Tiberian Trough is an example in history in which the strongly held beliefs and attitudes of one man delayed for an appreciable time the usually inevitable course of events and conditions.

THE CALIGULAN CHARGE
(A.D. 37–41)

If Tiberius was a penny-pincher and a miser, Caligula was the complete opposite. In his four years' reign, he commenced an extensive water supply program by starting two major aqueducts, the Claudia (6868 work units) and the Anio Novus (8688 work units). On a more personal side, he made significant expansions to the Domus Tiberiana, the imperial residence. Because of the speed with which he attacked these sophisticated projects, we can suspect that he pushed his projects as fast as was possible; the long period of little work under Tiberius would have reduced the major construction force available to him to a small cadre. We cannot judge the sophistication of his planning; we know that the aqueducts were needed but that was surely obvious to most public servants of the day. We dare not comment on the quality of his management; it takes little managerial skill to run as fast as possible on an obvious course. His reign was too short for us to judge him in the long run; both of his aqueducts, though started by him, had to be completed by Claudius after Caligula's death. At least he took steps to insure the water supply of his people; because of him, the Romans could at least drink and bathe.

One facet surprised us. By any sophisticated economic theory Caligula's charge should have resulted in inflation. Unless there were many potential workmen in the economy willing to work but not employed, the sudden demand for skilled workmen would have required that higher wages be paid to them or to their owners to get them to switch jobs. In turn, the tasks they left to join Caligula's projects would have had to be restaffed, and a place found from which to buy them away. This may be modern economics, but it is the kind of modern economics which was developed by watching unsophisticated economies in action. We are certain of the theory; two acceptable explanations are available. If we use the first explanation, there was significant unemployment in the Roman economy at the end of Tiberius' reign; alternatively, if we use the second explanation, there was inflation in the Caligulan economy, but there was no system to recognize it as such. In the first instance, there should have been

Aqua Claudia coming into Rome

some civil unrest before Caligula's period. We think that unrest would have been mentioned by one or more of the rather competent historians when they wrote of the period. Dio covers Tiberius only in abbreviation, but Suetonius and Tacitus give him standard coverage. They mention civil unrest but not to any great degree. Barbara Levick in her book on Tiberius says: "In A.D. 32 they (the plebs) were still able to make a vociferous demonstration in the theater for several days on end (it was over a grain shortage)."[15] For his part, Yavetz complains plaintively about the ingratitude of the plebs ". . . nor did the urban plebs show any gratitude towards him for his concern about public works, for the *congiaria* he gave the plebs, or for the measures he took to relieve the burden of debts."[16] Apparently they preferred cures to palliatives! On balance, we still prefer the explanation that inflation did occur under Tiberius' successor, but systems to track it did not exist.

THE CLAUDIAN CONNECTIONS
(A.D. 41–54)

Although Claudius had routinely to complete the two aqueducts started by Caligula, his other building programs were remarkably complex. They included two very innovative food supply oriented projects, projects which Augustus had feared to start, even though they had been first discussed by Julius Caesar. The two projects, the draining of the Fucine Lake and the creation of the harbor at Ostia, were not included in our earlier manpower study; they took a different kind of analysis and possibly some complex interrelationships between the two projects and other Claudian projects. For this reason, we have made a separate study of the two.

We will evaluate these two food projects in the following chapters and with that base we will evaluate the managerial skill of Claudius.

ENDNOTES TO CHAPTER IV

[1]Note how important H. B. Evans, "Agrippa's Water Plan," *American Journal of Archaelogy* 86 (1982), 411, considers Agrippa's planning of the aqueducts. He states "Not only did he lay the foundation for imperial administration of Rome's aqueduct system but his plan for water distribution was never entirely superseded."

Porta Praenestina, Rome

[2]The final step in the aqueduct restoration was not completed until A.D. 14 when the Aqua Julia was restored, creating an isolated peak at the very end of Augustus' reign. We believe that by this time the maintenance of the aqueducts was being carried on without interference from the Emperor or his senior advisors, a result arising from Agrippa's routinization of water-supply maintenance.

[3]*Roman Ostia* (Oxford, 1973), 54.

[4]"Si l'on en croit le scholiaste d'Horace, lui donna un commencement d'execution; mais la mort d'Agrippa suspendit l'enterprise." J. Carcopino, *Ostie* (Paris, 1919), 9.

[5]See also Z. Yavetz, *Plebs and Princeps* (Oxford, 1969), 13.

[6]An excellent discussion, which includes the modern view on this subject, can be found in Cosmo Rodewald, *Money in the Age of Tiberius* (Manchester, 1976), 1–17.

[7]*ESAR*, V, 36.

[8]Trans. by A. J. Church and W. J. Brodribb, *Complete Works of Tacitus*. The Modern Library (New York, 1942), 204–205.

[9]B. Levick, *Tiberius the Politician* (London, 1976), 133.

[10]"The Financial Crisis of 33 A.D.," *AJP* 56 (1935), 341.

[11]Cosmo Rodewald, *Money in the Age of Tiberius* (Manchester, 1976), 16.

[12]Harold Mattingly, *BMC* I (1976), cxxxii; Frank, *ESAR* V, 32.

[13]"Taxes and Trade in the Roman Empire," *JRS* 70 (1980), 107.

[14]Levick, 18.

[15]Levick, 122.

[16]Yavetz, 108.

To Rome (53 Miles) (88 Km)   (Avezzano)
                                LAKE FUCINE
                         Tunnel   Tunnel Entrance
          10 Km
Head of Aqueduct
                                River Liris
River Anio

Lake Fucine
and
Tunnel-Aqueduct Relationship

Scale 1:200000

Location of Lake
Fucine
in Roman Imperial
ITALY

English Miles

Principal roads ....

V. THE DRAINING OF THE FUCINE LAKE[1]

From A.D. 42 to A.D. 53 the emperor Claudius caused the Fucine Lake to be drained, according to Suetonius, "at a manpower cost of 30,000 men for eleven years" (*Claud*. 20.2–3). In the earlier chapters we established the relative public works manpower needs during this period in Rome; we developed this research only as a percentage variation of the manpower needs of each project compared to an arbitrary standard.[2] If the man-year figures for the Fucine Lake are accurate (330,000 man-years), we might use them as a method of translating the percentage-based data of our earlier work on Roman manpower into far more powerful absolute man-hours rather than to leave them in relative terms. We would be able to make the transfer because the underlying nature of the work in the draining of the Fucine Lake is nearly identical to some of the work required for building aqueducts—key Julio-Claudian projects.

Classicists and economic historians have long been interested in stating in absolute terms the economic statistics about this pivotal era in world history. For example, Duncan Jones, using a micro-approach, has developed unintegrated segments and isolated activities in absolute terms.[3] Tenney Frank, using a macro-approach, relied on Suetonius' Fucine Lake statement as an anchor in recreating the economic circumstances of the Claudian period.[4]

We showed earlier that there were striking peaks and valleys in the demand for labor, so big as to create possible political tension. (See Chart 1, Chapt. 2.) Our earlier calculations, however, were incomplete in that they did not cover two projects, the draining of the Fucine Lake and the Harbor at Ostia. These projects might have made important changes in the size of the manpower variability problem. In this chapter we partially remedy the first of these omissions.

Originally we limited the public work projects to the city of Rome and a circle of 60 kms. surrounding the city; we felt that the city's labor pool would not serve as a unitary market for more than 60 kms. from the center. We did, however, consider the aqueduct projects in their entirety even though some of their

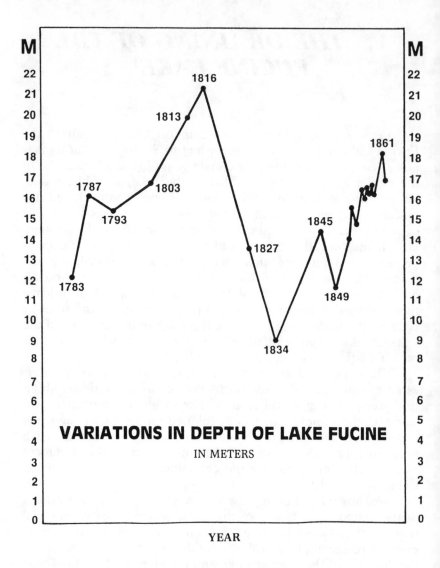

Chart. Variations in Depth of Lake Fucine

headwaters were beyond our circle. We now find that the Claudian and Anio Novus aqueducts come within about six miles of Claudius' major public works project at the Fucine Lake;[5] more important, we now recognize that the skills and tooling necessary for the upstream end of the two aqueducts are very similar to those used in draining the lake. We believe that artisans and supervisors working on one project were easily transferable to the other. Even more important, we believe that *conductores* bidding on part of one project might, if their work backlogs needed it, bid on part of the other. Accordingly, after quantifying the workload involved in the Fucine Lake, we then discuss the modifications or the amplifications needed to our earlier work to allow for this possible expansion of the natural market for Roman city labor.

THE LAKE

The Fucine Lake, located at an altitude of 2100 feet above sea level, 53 miles east of Rome, was fed by rain and by melting snow from the Appennines. Since it had no natural surface outlet, its water level varied by balancing its inflows with its losses by evaporation and by heavy underground seepage. The level varied gradually but dramatically in an irregular cycle lasting for decades from peak to peak. For example (from modern data):

Year		
depth in	1783	was 43 feet
depth in	1816	was 74 feet
depth in	1835	was 31 feet
depth in	1861	was 61 feet[6]

On the average the lake covered 37,000 acres but since it had a gradually sloping bottom, its area varied remarkably. For example, between 1816 and 1835 we calculate that the water retreated four miles, uncovering productive farmland, only to take much of it back again 26 years later.[7] We know that, because of the continuous rise and fall of the lake, the Marsi, inhabitants of the area, asked Augustus to make an outlet for it (Suet. *Claud.* 20.1). Although both Augustus and, earlier, Julius Caesar had refused the Marsian request, Claudius constructed a drainage tunnel; Nero neglected it; Trajan and Hadrian cleaned it out; then almost everybody ignored it until 1835.[8] In 1876 one of the chief engineers, Brisse, sponsored by Prince Torlonia, finally

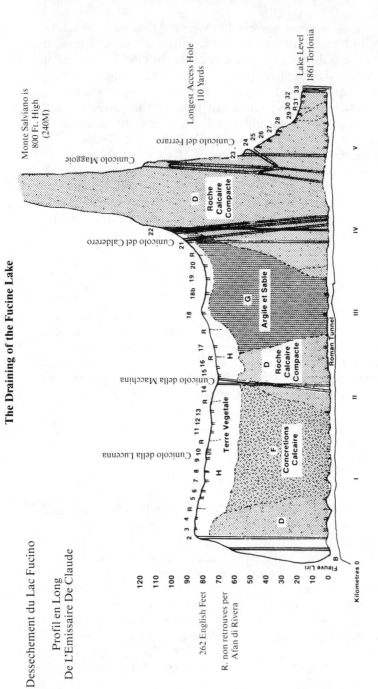

The Draining of the Fucine Lake

Dessechement du Lac Fucino

Profil en Long
De L'Emissaire De Claude

Source: Brisse, Plate IV

Echelle des Longueurs 0^m,00005 pour L'Metre
Echelle des Hauteurs 0^m.001 pour L'Metre

Mount Salviano

retunnelled on Claudius' path with a doubled cross section.[9] Today the former lake bottom is a pleasant, highly fertile plain.

THE PROJECT

Claudius had the lake drained into the River Liris through a tunnel over three miles in length (6180 yds.) and nearly one thousand feet under Mount Salviano.

From an engineering point of view the work is remarkable only for its size. Roman—and before them, Greek and Egyptian—mining had developed the basic techniques and engineering competence.[10] Tunneling over long stretches was common in previous aqueduct construction near Rome. The Romans understood and managed the problems of rock hardness, of variations in soil consistency and of ventilation, without recourse to innovative techniques. Thus, the draining of a lake, while a major task, represented no technological breakthrough, nor should it be regarded as remarkable except for its size and its cost.[11] (Meiggs maintains that the construction of the Harbor of Ostia was a larger project.)[12]

THE ANALYSIS

To test the accuracy of Suetonius' statement that 30,000 men worked continuously for eleven years, we had to determine: (1) the nature and size of the task (2) the size of the crews (3) the daily output per crew and (4) the number of shifts worked per day.

The Nature and Size of the Task

The digging crew constructed a tunnel (6180 yards long with a cross section of 11.9 square yards) by sinking 40 vertical shafts (14.16 feet × 14.16 feet in cross section) along a previously surveyed path down to the level required (an average of 196 feet). Then half of each crew dug horizontally upstream and the other half downstream until they met the crews from the two adjoining shafts.[13] Thus, the crews built the tunnel in segments, possibly simultaneously, attacked from 40 main shafts. There could, however, be no more than 40 crews working in the tunnel at one time.

The 40 main shafts required ventilation shafts, dug at an angle, to provide the air necessary to support the workers in the main tunnel.[14] These *cuniculi* (from the Italian word meaning

Corinthian painted *Pinax* (ca. 550 BC) showing miners working in a confined space "rabbit holes") were two times as long in cumulative total length as the tunnel and the main shafts were.[15] When the *cuniculi* crews are added to the main shaft crews, there could have been no more than 120 crews.

Size of the Crews

Next, it is necessary to calculate the maximum number of men needed in each crew. Fortunately, here we are well supplied with hard archaeological facts. In 1854 when the Roman tunnel, plugged for centuries, was reopened, Brisse reports all the details necessary for a mathematical study of the draining of the lake. He provides us with the dimensions of the tunnel—length, breadth and height; he tells us the number of shafts that were used; he gives us the number of ventilation holes ancillary to the main shafts that were used as well as the work methods used, the nature of the rocks encountered and even a report of the accidents which occurred in Claudius' time. In addition, the extensive data on Roman mining permit us to make reasonable estimates of the amount of rock a miner can dislodge in a day. (Remember mining and tunneling require the same basic skills.) The severe space constraints in which the work had to be performed removed any options as to the size of the crew; for example, the available digging space in the tunnel was approximately eight feet wide—no more than two men with tools can work simultaneously on one face in such a restricted area. Given this key piece of data, we can determine the size of the crew. We have placed the details of our actual calculations in the Appendix 3. From these calculations we have established the crew size as follows:

Digging Crew Size
(Each crew worked on one shaft plus two tunnel faces)

Face Men[16]	4
Spoil Collectors	2
Porters to lift	4
Lift bucket loaders	2
Capstan men[17]	4
Bucket unloaders	2
Utility men	2
	20 men[18]

The figures are not subject to much error. Numbers are constrained by space and by the amount of work a man can be expected to do. Failure of a crew to do its daily task would almost certainly result only in delay of the job or in the use of a new crew on a second shift rather than in the expansion of the original crew. Ancient sources and archaeological evidence support many of our assumptions (see Appendix 3).

These figures represent a crew size in its most intensive labor phase after the shaft has been sunk and while work is underway on the two tunnel faces. While the shaft is being sunk, the work force would be slightly smaller. We have assumed an equal crew size in the *cuniculi* sinking. Since the *cuniculi* were cut into a shaft at a slant from the surface, they required only one face. Thus, although there were a smaller number of face-men needed, more workers were involved in the manual labor of lifting the detritus up a rather steep incline to the surface.

The Daily Output Per Crew

Mining sources have provided us with a variety of data on the amount of rock a man could be expected to remove from a mine face in a day. Unfortunately, the sources do not agree. We list in Table 1 below a summary of output-predictions based on the four principal sources. The table calculates the time required to excavate the longest shaft in the Fucine Lake project, Shaft #22. The data is provided under one, two, or three shifts per day modes. Since data are usually calculated on "a 9 to 10 hour day" the three shift figures assume 8 hour days.

We cannot accept the estimate of Ardaillon since, even with shifts, the workers could not finish the required work in the eleven years allotted for the job by Suetonius. Hopper agrees that Ardaillon's estimate is too slow.[19]

The fourth authority, Davies, believes that progress would be extremely fast, and his estimates have been strongly criticized on this account.[20] So rapid would be progress at Davies' rate that the whole project could have been done in less than two years.

The remaining two estimates, by Bromehead and by Forbes, fit well into our eleven year envelope. Forbes says that his data are "from inscriptions" (without a footnote). Bromehead says that "it has been calculated" (again without a footnote). The rate of progress is obviously only an estimate and would always vary greatly depending on the difficulty of the rock being attacked and the working conditions involved. We accept the Bromehead/Forbes estimate. From our point of view, a higher or lower rate per day would not change the manpower needs—except to change

Table 1
Shaft #22
Time to Complete under Different Assumptions

Authority	Cu. Ft. removed in one 9–10 hr. Shift: 2 face-men	in One Shift	in Two Shifts	in Three Shifts
Ardaillon	3.06	41.47 yrs.	20.7 yrs.	13.8 yrs.
Bromehead	30.14	4.23 yrs.	2.11 yrs.	1.6 yrs.
Forbes	30.14	4.23 yrs.	2.11 yrs.	1.6 yrs.
Davies	98.4	1.29 yrs.	.65 yrs.	.41 yrs.

Shaft 22 is 400 ft. deep with a cross section of 14.16 x 14.16 feet; 4 face men 14.16 x 14.16 x 400 = 80202 cu. feet to remove.

Notes and Sources:

Edouard Ardaillon: *Les Mines du Laurion dans L'Antiquite* (Paris, 1897) 31: 12 cm x 60 cm; two hours for a good worker = 8640 cm^3 ten hr. shift; 8640 x 5 = 43200 cm^3 ÷ 28316 cm^3/ft^3 = 1.53 ft^3/ shift 2 men per face, 1.5 x 2 = 3.06 ft^3 per shift.

C. N. Bromehead: "Mining and Quarrying to the Seventeenth Century" in *History of Technology*, Charles Singer, et al., editors, II (Oxford, 1956): "Shafts were regular, about 1.9 x 1.3 rectangular," and "it has been calculated that in shaft sinking a miner averaged 4.5 meters per month," p. 3 (1.9 x 39.37/12) x (1.3 x 39.37/12) x (4.5 x 39.37/12) = 392 ft^3/month, 392 ÷ 26 day month = 15.07; for 2 men, 30.14 ft^3/day.

R. J. Forbes: *Studies in Ancient Technology* (Leiden, 1966): "We hear from inscriptions that a miner averaged 4.5m per month," p. 153; "Rectangular section, 1.9 x 1.3," p. 152. Same as Bromehead.

Oliver Davies: *Roman Mines in Europe* (Oxford, 1935) 31: 1.9m x 1.3m (The shaft cross section not stated—we calculated using Bromehead's cross section. [see above]) x 30m^3 = 6.23 ft x 4.26 ft x 98.4 ft. = 2612 ft^3 per month, 2 men 2612/26 = 100.5 ft^3 per 2 men per day.

the slack between a perfect job and a realistic one—unless an acceptable elapsed time could be achieved only with shift work, thus doubling or tripling the number of crews involved. We discuss this possibility in Table 1.

The Number of Shifts Worked Per Day

The evidence shows that the ancient practice on the use of shifts was not consistent. Gustave Glotz concludes that "At Laurion each shift did ten hours' work after ten hours' rest."[21] According to Pliny, shifts were used in gold mining in Spain. He states: ". . . Long galleries excavated into the mountain. The lamps measure the shifts and the men may not see daylight for months on end" (*NH* 33.70). On the other hand, Davies, speaking also of Spain, says: "the only lamp niches near the adit-mouths at Linares were round corners" as proof that there were not shifts. Nighttime operations would have required additional lamps beyond the corners. Furthermore, he notes that in a Portuguese environment: "the bath was open for men from the eighth hour of the day to the second of the night, proving there was no system of shifts, but all miners started at dawn and came off in the afternoon."[22]

The decision to operate in shifts is a managerial one: thus, we would expect shifts to be used when it was profitable to do so. For example, Hopper notes that at Laurion there was prodigal deployment of labor on the part of miners concerned to make as much profit as possible . . . the time factor is an important one in view of the length and nature of the leases.[23] At Laurion prospects were sold by the *poletae* for ten years and working mines for three (Aristotle, *Ath. Pol.* 47). Obviously shifts would maximize the profit made for a specified lease period.

We can see no *obvious reason* why management would have operated the Fucine Lake project on a multi-shift basis *as a policy*. On the other hand, there are *good reasons* why management would have used shift operation *as an emergency or a work balancing system*. The tunnel was subject to water problems; an upstream shaft and tunnel would collect water, and the only practical way to get rid of it was to drain it down the tunnel. Thus, it was urgent that management keep the downstream portions of the tunnel on schedule; if it did not, it would catch up by using shifts. Otherwise upstream crews would be idle awaiting drainage. Brisse encountered such problems in the modern cleanout and expansion.[24]

Because shafts varied in length and in difficulty of the rock involved, we can expect that the project director had to adjust workloads constantly.[25] There can be little doubt that management initially shifted crews from the upstream shafts to downstream shafts; then, later, downstream crews aided by earlier priority and easier digging would have been available to help out as the project neared completion. It should be noted that, because of space constraints, additional men could not be added to a shaft or the tunnel without the use of a second shift. As a result we believe that there was a significant amount of shift work on the Fucine project but that it generally was provided by using regular first shift crews on second shifts when they would otherwise have been temporarily unemployed. Thus, we do not believe that shift work could have added to the total number of men employed.

We encountered references to "nine to ten hour shifts," or to working "ten hours on and ten hours off" or, to "10 Stunden (Schichtdauer)" in the mining literature.[26] Because of this we believe that three shift operations were not considered.

QUANTITATIVE DIRECT LABOR AND TIME SUMMARY

From the above calculations we can draw together a summary of the direct labor requirements of the Fucine Lake project. We have calculated with considerable confidence:

There were 40 main shafts and 80 *cuniculi* shafts, 120 in all.
There were 20 men per crew.
$120 \times 20 = 2400$ workers.

A maximum of 2400 workers could have been employed at any one time directly on digging and on detritus disposal. There will be manpower needs for facing, for timbering, and for providing special support in difficult areas. These, however, will either be needed after completion of a task or will require that work be stopped while repair or shoring takes place.

Besides the basic crew, another important worker is a bricklayer. Since the Romans excavated 3518 yds. through compact rock without revetments, bricklayers would be needed only for 2662 yds. of the tunnel[27] and not constantly since the diggers progressed only 3.36 in. per day on each face.[28] In addition, at

some time during the construction it was necessary to build the
hydraulic system which controlled the flow of water from the
lake into the tunnel. This consisted of three concrete and brick
gates and a set of dams needed to create two small ponds used
as buffers against turbulence on the lake proper.[29] Timing of these
constructions may have been critical, but the total man-days
needed was modest considering the overall task. At other times
the bricklayers must have been assigned other tasks such as
timbering. To allow for these special tasks, we have added two
hundred additional men. Besides the crew members and the
bricklayers, there must also have been at least some supervisors.
We have assumed that first line supervision is included in each
of the crews.

   These workers should be the main ones involved in the direct
labor of the draining of the Fucine Lake. As a comparison for
this figure we should note that Brisse, while using methods available in the 19th century, dug his more modern tunnel which
required four times as much rock removal as the ancient Roman
one with the help of approximately 2000 men.[30]

Minimum Completion Time Under Ideal Conditions

Given: 11,921,689 ft.^{3} rock to be removed
                     30 ft.^{3} per face per day
                        160   working faces

   If we assume 316 workdays per year,[31] it would take 7.9
years to complete the project. The Romans undoubtedly did not
finish the project in eight years. There would have been failure
of phasing and lack of coordination, if nothing else, to delay the
completion. It should be noted, however, that the use of extensive partial second shift operations would have reduced these
phasing and coordination problems and minimized the time
required.

IMPACT OF ACCIDENTS AND EMERGENCY PROBLEMS

   In our analysis of manpower needs for the draining of the
lake we presented it as an uncomplicated task, without unexpected problems. In a project such as this one, emergencies or

unexpected developments were certain to occur. It is necessary, thus, to evaluate the impact of typical crisis events on manpower needs. We will discuss these by type:

Slips, Cave-Ins and Tunnel Collapses

Since the work is spread into a large number of different work places, crises such as slips will impact no more than one or two work places immediately. At these work places, regular work will cease until the crisis is resolved.[32] In most cases, the work force will be the same, but in some cases, specialist help will be brought in. This help would be few in numbers, would probably be taken from a different existing crew, and would displace workers on the original crew. Presumably, regular work would cease while decisions and *ad hoc* corrections were underway. In terms of men employed the immediate manpower-costs would be negligible; in terms of total manpower costs, it would increase the length of time the force would be needed but not the size of this force.

Water

Water problems (probably very serious ones, for example, standing water in shafts) were inevitable. Brisse in his enlargement found the rock so severely water-logged (frequently from above, not down the old tunnel) as to threaten the project; the Romans would have faced a similar problem. After a futile attempt at baling (1 bucket of spoil for 9 of water),[33] the Brisse group did the obvious—it waited until the downstream end of the tunnel drained the water away—the only rational solution to the water problem. Thus, water, while a serious problem, would result only in delay, not in the employment of more manpower. We have earlier discussed management's use of shifts to resolve such problems.

Epidemics

Sickness would merely delay the completion or temporarily increase the number of men involved. We include two men (about ten percent) for routine daily ineffectives.

Our conclusion is that labor force size would not be significantly changed by crises; the length of time the force was used would be affected.

INDIRECT LABOR

In addition to the regular crew, there would be some support labor: guards, limeburners, tool makers, brickmakers, wood-cutters, and transporters. The Aljustrel Tables (A.D. 117–138) suggest that bath managers and employees, fullers, shoemakers, and barbers would have been covered by managerial regulations at an isolated site such as the Fucine area.[34]

A modern labor force requires machines and/or animals, both of which necessitate special management. The Romans, on the other hand, seem not to have used animals directly[35] and only a limited range of machines. Without the physical remains of buildings it is difficult to estimate how large this support force was. A major difficulty involves uncertainty as to the degree of vertical integration which existed. Thus, we presume that wood-cutting, lime burning and brickmaking were a portion of the basic on-location work force and that local blacksmiths made tools from the iron blooms which were an item of normal trade at the time (Varro, *RR* 1. 16.4).[36] We presume that personal support (food services, shelter management and clothing) were the responsibility of the individual; these overhead activities would not be included in the work force. If the indirect labor was supporting, as we believe it was, a direct labor force of around 3,000 men, then it is difficult to believe that as many as 30,000 men were needed for the drainage operation. If this were so, every man in the digging would have nine men offering him support.

Project estimators today use ratios to calculate support labor based on direct labor base—the U.S. military used to say that it takes 10 men to support one rifleman—but in the Fucine Lake case we are confounded by our doubts as to the degree of vertical integration involved. Generally, a ratio of 9 indirect to 1 direct seems too heavy a support force; a 2 to 1 seems too light. A ratio of 5:1 would mean that 15,000 men were involved.

The experience of Brisse in his reboring and in his enlarging the same Roman tunnel in 1854 provides only low-credibility data. The technological environment was quite different. However, he used approximately 2000 men including direct, indirect and associated with the project.[37] Given an equal "direct to support" labor ratio, Brisse would have used but 200 direct laborers, an inappropriately small number. Differences in the environment between the two eras would generally replace direct labor with support labor at the later date.

CONCLUSIONS

We conclude with a high degree of confidence that the project took eleven years. Our estimate of 7.9 years if everything is perfect makes eleven years a logical, real-life result. The time involved would have been public knowledge; Suetonius would hardly be incorrect to such an extent on this dimension.

We have grave doubts about the accuracy of Suetonius' claim that 30,000 men were continuously used. We have a high degree of confidence in our calculation of just under 3000 direct laborers. Suetonius' figure might be defended under the following circumstances:

1. if Suetonius included in the labor force not only the indirect labor cost but also all the bookkeepers, harlots and priests that would gather around such a permanently established force. These might even include farmers, weavers and millers since this was essentially a semi-subsistence economy.

2. if the word "continuously" (*continuis*) in Suetonius has been mistranslated. *Continuis* has two meanings, with reference to a person it means "assiduous;" otherwise it means "continuous." It is an adjective, thus the meaning cannot be "worked continuously." It could in English modify only "men," thus meaning "assiduous men." The Latin grammar is more complex and is discussed in the footnote.[38]

3. if the number 30,000 represented all the men who worked and included the workers on the conduit canals, open cuts extending for miles in the dried lake bed in a wide network. There is no physical reason why a very large number of men might not have been employed if the need were high enough to hire additional men for a short time. The later Brisse project provides a photograph of rows of men working with shovels as their only tool on the conduit canal, an open feeder canal stretching from directly in front of the camera to the far horizon in the background.[39]

4. if Suetonius used 30,000 merely as an indication of a large number e.g. in English as "a thousand and one reasons."

5. if the 30,000 employed had been a padding of the payroll—a possibility which Agrippina believed when she accused Narcissus of greed and of fraud (Tac. *Ann.* 12.57).

6. if the managers of the project had intentionally staffed up to a full two shifts on a permanent basis. In this case, however, we believe it would have been inevitable that many crews would have been idle for long periods while problems (water, slips, phasing discontinuities) were resolved.

We conclude that the employment of 30,000 men for eleven years in digging the tunnel cannot be used to translate relative terms into absolute terms. While the study of the Fucine Lake did not provide a chance to change the "relative manpower costs" of our earlier city of Rome study into absolute man hours, it did suggest some fascinating possibilities.

The Fucine lake project is only a few kilometers from the headwater of the Claudia and Anio Novus aqueducts. Almost certainly these water projects were built sequentially, starting at the source and finishing 70 kilometers later in the city of Rome.

The earlier (but not later) portions of the aqueduct require almost exactly the same kind of engineering and construction work as did the Fucine Lake. The timing of the two projects was:

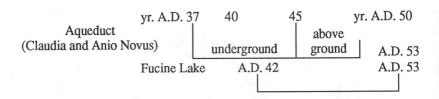

Some possibilities:

1. The planners for the Fucine Lake project had learned or had honed their trade in planning the aqueducts.

2. The *conductores* actually building the Fucine Lake tunnel were veterans of the aqueducts' earlier phases.

3. The labor force on the Fucine Lake and that on the two aqueducts worked for the same *conductores*, who moved them back and forth as needed. It might, therefore, be that Suetonius' figures included both forces as part of the Fucine Lake force—another possible explanation of the discrepancy between our estimate of the work force and Suetonius' statement.

Some speculations:

1. Claudius initiated the Fucine Lake project because of the availability of nearby (soon to be unemployed) technical and managerial workers skilled in water management.

2. The emperor recognized that he could use in winter, on the Fucine Lake, men who could not work during that season (the concrete froze) on the aqueducts (Front. *Aq.* 2.123).

TRANSLATION OF GENERAL DATA INTO ABSOLUTE TERMS

It is difficult to compare the economic effort involved in two separate projects if the projects are undertaken in different environments. We decided to limit our evaluation of the man-power costs of Roman public works to relative rather than ab-solute figures because we were uncertain how much infrastruc-ture cost should go to each project. Thus, who made the tools? Who quarried the marble? Who made the cement? A work group, constructing its own tools and even smelting its own iron, would use much more manpower than one buying most of its raw ma-terials from an outside source.

In the Julio-Claudian public construction study we finessed this problem by presuming the same ratio of support to direct cost would obtain in all studied projects. This assumption was reasonable so long as all projects were completed in the same basic environment. Our figures are defensible in this earlier study because we limited it to the city and its environs. A brickworks in this area presumably would be able to provide merchant bricks (bricks sold from stock to any buyer) to any project anywhere within the studied region.

Although the Fucine Lake is no more than 10 miles outside the area which we studied in our original Julio-Claudian work, we are uncomfortable with an assumption that the infrastructure supporting the Fucine Lake project bears much resemblance to that within the Roman region. Before the draining of the Fucine Lake the country of the Marsi was sparsely populated, rough and uncivilized; transport across the few miles was extremely difficult: mountains, gorges, valley and hills intervened.[40]

If we are to use our primarily direct labor calculations as a bridge into the aqueduct construction projects of the original Julio-Claudian study, we must make assumptions about the rel-ative degree of vertical integration in the Fucine Lake area as opposed to that in Rome. It is possible that the apparently dis-torted manpower needs of Suetonius are a result of a major investment of manpower in infrastructure, manpower not nor-mally required in a city project.

We believe that the translation project is possible; however, much further research needs to be done into the kinds of support available to Fucine Lake workmen. It is conceivable that our ancient sources might have included within their cost even the agricultural effort expended in growing their own food supply.

Our visits and research on the region of the Marsi were insufficient to give us insight into this missing link in our efforts to generate absolute data. We believe this to have a high priority for new research in this potentially rewarding area.

ENDNOTES TO CHAPTER V

[1]A version of this chapter, "The Draining of the Fucine Lake: A Quantitative Analysis," reprinted with permission, appeared in *The Ancient World* 12 (1985), 105–120.

[2]Thorntons, "Manpower Needs for the Public Works Programs of the Julio-Claudian Emperors," *Journal of Economic History* XLIII, No. 2 (June, 1983), 373–378.

[3]See pp. 156–162 for prices in Italy in Richard Duncan-Jones, *The Economy of the Roman Empire* (Cambridge, 1974).

[4]*ESAR*, V, 42.

[5]Map, Istituto Geografico Militare, #F5063 and Frontinus 1.14–15.

[6]Alexander Brisse and Leon de Retrou, *The Draining of the Fucine Lake* (Rome, 1876), 8–9 (hereafter referred to as Brisse).

[7]Brisse, 8–9.

[8]Frederic II in 1239 and Alfonso I of Aragon in the 15th century seemed to have made efforts to clean out the channel.

[9]Brisse, 239–242 and Plate V.

[10]John F. Healy, *Mining and Metallurgy in the Greek and Roman World* (London, 1978), 70–102; Oliver Davies, *Roman Mines in Europe* (Oxford, 1935), 16–38 and Edouard Ardaillon, *Les Mines du Laurion* (Paris, 1897), 20–58.

[11]An example of a similar earlier work is the draining of Lake Copais in Boeotia. See J. G. Frazer's commentary on Pausanias (London, 1898), 117, where he reports on an attempt, apparently not successful, to drain the Copaic Lake. For a modern account of the drainage consult M. Kambanis, "Le dessechement du lac Copais par les anciens," *Bulletin de Correspondence Hellenique* (1893), 333 ff.

[12]Russell Meiggs, *Roman Ostia* (Oxford, 1973), 54.

[13]Brisse, 18.

[14]Brisse, 23.

[15]Brisse, 16.

[16]C. N. Bromehead, "Mining and Quarrying to the Seventeenth Century," in *History of Technology,* ed. by Charles Singer et al. (Oxford, 1956), 2, Fig. 1.

[17]Ch. Daremberg et E. Saglio, *Dictionnaire des Antiquités Grecques et Romaines*, 602, Fig. 2662.

[18]A stone bas-relief from Linares, first or second century A.D., shows a mining crew of eight miners and a foreman en route to their work on a face. This is basically the size we are suggesting for our crews since our crews are working on two faces. The bas-relief is reproduced in C. N. Bromehead, "Mining and Quarrying," 9 and Joan Liversidge, *Everyday Life in the Roman Empire* (London and New York, 1976), 120.

[19]"The Laurion Mines: A Reconsideration," *Annual of the British School at Athens* 63 (1968), 318.

[20]Hopper, 318.

[21]Gustave Glotz, *Ancient Greece at Work, An Economic History of Greece from the Homeric Period to the Roman Conqueror* (New York, 1926), 280.

[22]Davies, 12.

[23]Hopper, 318.

[24]Brisse, 101.

[25]See shaft 19, Brisse, 101–102.

[26]Ardaillon, 25; Glotz, 280; Siegfried Lauffer, "Die Bergwerkssklaven von Laureion," *Akademie der Wissenschaften und der Literatur* I (Wiesbaden, 1955, NR. 12), 1124.

[27]Brisse, 94; 139.

[28]Bromehead, 3; R. J. Forbes, *Studies in Ancient Technology,* Vol. VII (Leiden, 1966), 153. The methods used in tunnel digging are identical to those used in Roman mining, an operation which is extensively documented. See note 9. Some additional books are: Friedrich Klemm, trans. by Dorothea Waley Singer, *A History of Western Technology* (New York, 1959); Thomas A. Rickard, *Man and Metals: A History of Mining,* 2 vols. (New York, 1932).

[29]Brisse, 32–33.

[30]Brisse, 121.

[31]A. K. Michels, *Calendar of the Roman Republic* (1967), 68.

[32]Brisse, 35.

[33]Brisse, 99.

[34]Salvatore Riccobono (ed.), *Fontes Iuris Romani Antejustiniani* (Florence, 1941–1949), no. 105, 502; *CIL* 2, p. 788, n. 5181; see Healy, fig. 32 for a reproduction of part of the bronze plaques known as the Aljustrel Tables.

[35]Brisse, 20.

[36]Forbes, "Metallurgy" in *History of Technology,* ed. by Charles Singer et al. (Oxford, 1956), 59; Davies, 6–7.

[37]Brisse, 121.

[38]Let us examine the Latin adjective *continuus*: it has two meanings — it means "continuous" when it refers to periods of time but "assiduous and unremitting" when it refers to men (Tac. *Ann.* 11.5). Since the adjective is in the ablative case, technically it would seem because of proximity to modify "milibus;" then its meaning would be: a continuous 30,000 men. But since "hominum" is a partitive genitive (because any word used with the plural of "mille" is automatically in the genitive case) "continuis" can be translated as: 30,000 hard working men. In this case it would not tell us anything about the continuity of the work.

[39]E. Agostinoni, *Il Fucino* (Bergamo, 1908), 43.

[40]T. A. Rickard talks about a similar environment in Spain: "The mines were in the heart of the mountains, in a region that was forlorn

and forsaken and in one where a large population could not be maintained except by making careful provision for sundry social services.'' ''Mining of the Romans in Spain,'' *Journal of Roman Studies* 18 (1928), 139.

VI. THE HARBOR OF OSTIA

Although Claudius demonstrated ingenuity in draining the Fucine Lake to solve a part of Rome's food problem and to ease his labor management problems, we need not give him too much credit for his start of the harbor of Ostia. He was compelled to do so by the threat of famine. Seneca tells us that there was only eight days' supply of wheat available (Sen. *Brev. Vit.* 18.5; see also Orosius 7.6.17) when Claudius began his reign. On the other hand, he might have settled for a less difficult solution. He was amply warned by others of the risks that he was taking: the cost of construction would be high and the position of Ostia at the mouth of the river would lead to the danger of silting (Vitr. 5.12.1). Dio, too, reports that the architects involved in the decision were extremely pessimistic, so much so that they were believed to have intentionally exaggerated the difficulties (40.11.3). The decision seems to have attracted all the amateur planners, too. Quintilian, in his manual for orators says: "When the building of the harbor of Ostia was debated, it was not for the orator to give his opinion, it was the calculation of the architect that was needed" (Quint. *Inst.* 2.21.18).

As was so often the case, Caesar originated the harbor proposal. He had three parts to his plan: first for the harbor itself, second, for a canal from Ostia to Terracina with a provision for a protected water route from one city to the other and, finally, for draining the Pomptine marshes to provide fertile land (Plut. *Caes.* 58.10). Caesar eventually abandoned both the canal and the harbor projects because of their difficulty. Claudius, adopting the harbor project, left the canal and the marshes for Nero to toy with.

The port problem which had become so serious by Claudius' reign had been a long time in coming. The harbor did not create Rome; Rome created the harbor. Rome, unlike so many ancient cities, did not develop from a communication and a transport hub; originally, she was a local power who fed herself from her own agricultural output. Thus, when she outgrew her subsistence sources, she found herself very poorly supplied with easy solutions. The mouth of the Tiber could never be a satisfactory

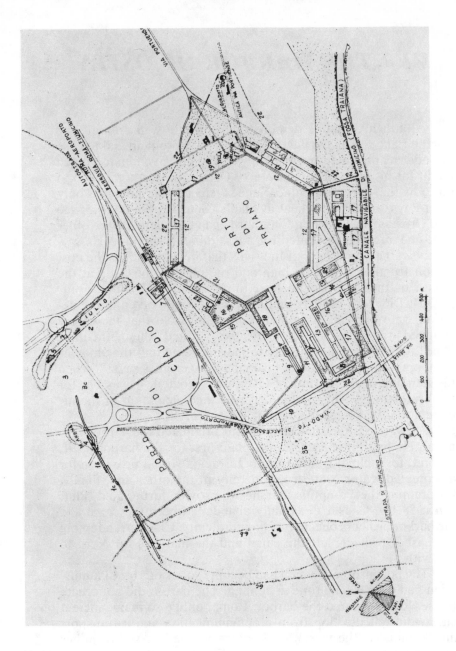

Ports of Claudius and Trajan

funnel through which to pour food for the world's capital. To make matters worse, she had abused her native sources: she had failed to supply the manpower to maintain her drainage system in the Volscian Plain and had turned over the farms of the rich to grazing. What had once been a productive agricultural area was transformed into the dismal Pomptine Marshes (Pliny, *NH* 3.59). Plutarch comments that the formerly fruitful, cultivated area of Etruria, once an important source of grain for Rome, was in decline; Tiberius Gracchus found the land deserted (Plut. *Gracchi,* 8.9).

Even as early as the second century B.C. Rome was relying heavily on grain from Sicily, from Sardinia, from Carthage and from Numidia (Livy 33.42.8; 36.2.12; 36.4.5). Before Claudius' project, Rome used two ports to import most of the foreign goods into the city. The river mouth at Ostia was the first of these two; its advantage was the elimination of almost all of the land transport. Water transport is essential for integrated widely scattered empires; Rome was the first to develop such an empire successfully. It was far easier to transport by water from most ports in the empire than to transport the same goods by land from rural Italy. Much of the deterioration and much of the abandonment of fertile Italian land resulted from competition from farther distant sources which could rely on all-water transport. We can understand the development of the Roman Empire's transportation system in the light of this important fact: Egypt is closer to Rome, considered from a cost viewpoint, than is the upper Po valley, or even inland Etruria. Mare Nostrum was not a boast; it was an economic statement. Thus, the Ostian port was by far the cheapest way to Rome.

The principal alternate port was at Puteoli on the Bay of Naples. Puteoli was unquestionably the safer and better appointed port; its weakness was the long haul north to Rome. Given that the natural river harbor at Ostia could not handle all the trade, it is an economic fact that the trade would have been distributed based on weight and volume, and, to the degree that governments could influence it, on the strategic importance of the goods involved. Food was bulky, of low "value to weight" ratio, and of high strategic importance. Thus, the Tiber mouth tended to specialize in food. Because it could not handle all the food, however, significant portions of the grain trade (primarily the big Alexandrian freighters) (Sen. *Ep.* 77.1–2) still came in to Puteoli and were transshipped north by land, or, to bypass the jam-up at the actual river end, reloaded at Puteoli into smaller vessels which, after sailing north, could go straight up the Tiber to the city proper.[1]

Technological progress increased the problems which tradesmen experienced in using the river port. With the growth in the size of merchantmen and with the growing importance of Egypt, whose cargoes were transported in the larger ships, the sand bars at the mouth of the Tiber became increasingly risky. As a result, these large ships were kept outside the harbor and their cargoes transferred into lighters which could go directly to the city of Rome. While this double handling was not necessarily more costly (it saved the shifting *inside* the harbor to river lighters), it was dangerous in heavy weather (Strabo, 231–2).

THE HARBOR

Ostia is situated at the mouth of the Tiber about 15 miles almost directly west of Rome. Aside from the river mouth, which is subject to silting, as most river mouths are, there is near Ostia no solid natural feature which could have served as the basis for protection from the weather. Most high quality harbors possess a set of promontories serving as bases from which to construct moles; these moles then encircle a segment of sea of adequate depth. The west coast of Italy in the region of Ostia is alluvial, without rocky outcrops; the shore is sandy and devoid of permanent features. This topography is forbidding to harbor builders and could be blamed for the reluctance of architects and of engineers to attempt a harbor there. Given a requirement to build a harbor, regardless of the problems, the builders can approach the task in two ways: First, they could build moles from the shore perpendicularly out into the ocean from two anchors, spaced an adequate distance apart; at a sufficient distance out, the moles will be curved toward each other, enclosing an adequate area of the sea. If such a shore is gently shelving, a large amount of dredging within the enclosed area will be required.

A second approach is to build a wall along the shore on the land edge and then dig out from behind the wall an adequate amount of the shore to make a man-dug lake of the proper size. After the digging is completed, the wall is pierced to let in the water and to make an entrance for vessels.[2]

The harbor at Ostia seems to have been a composite of the two. Apparently, about two miles north of the Tiber's mouth a sand spit naturally occurred, jutting out into the open sea.[3]

Any marine engineer worth his salt will recognize that such a project is a daunting one; reputations will be lost by anyone accepting such a charge!

THE PROJECT

We have substantial, relatively new information about the actual dimensions and the construction details of the Claudian harbor; the excavations incident to the construction during 1957–1960 of Leonardo da Vinci airport assisted us to a better understanding of Claudius' plan. At the time of the construction, care was taken to document some of the details of the Claudian harbor before they disappeared beneath the airport. According to Otello Testaguzza, the engineer who documented the research:

> Claudius' port was more or less circular, with occasional indentations. Its area was almost one-third of a square mile, and its maximum diameter over half a mile (a thousand meters). Its north and east sides were somewhat flattened and were the sites of the two moles pictured on Nero's coin, described in our ancient sources respectively as the left-hand mole (plan, 1a-c, 4) . . . and the right-hand mole (plan, 5, 2), . . . the latter fitted with harbor facilities. The entrance to the harbor lay between the two incurving ends of these moles (plan, 3).[4]

He also provides us with a diagram of the Claudian harbor, corrected for the latest information developed from the Airport Archaeological Project mentioned above.

THE ANALYSIS

Informed by the statements of Suetonius and Dio, we believe that the Harbor at Ostia is a composite both of "digging out the sand" and of "building a wall." Suetonius (*Claud.* 20.3) states:

> He constructed a harbour at Ostia. Two encircling arms were built out to sea: at the entrance where the water was deep a breakwater was added. In order to provide more secure foundations for this breakwater he first sank the ship which had brought the great obelisk from Egypt . . . above he set a very high tower on the model of the Alexandrian Pharos, so that ships could steer their course by its burning light at night.

Dio (40.11.4), however, differs slightly in his statement:

> First he excavated a not inconsiderable area of land: he built a retaining

ASSUMPTION
(Chart 2)

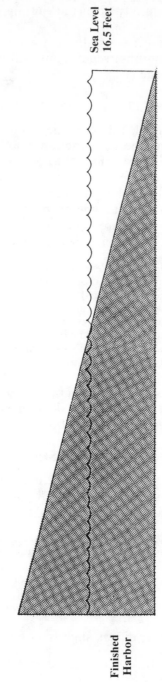

Chart 2. Harbor of Ostia

wall right round this excavated area and then let the sea come in. Next, in the sea itself he built great moles, one on each side, enclosing a large expanse of sea. He formed an island in the sea and built on it a tower with a beacon.[5]

Testaguzza's on site investigation verifies that it was primarily a digging job rather than a dredging one: "It was completely man-made, carved out of terra firma. . . ."[6] We have, however, irrefutable information that at least a portion of the excavation was made through dredging of an area that was originally under water: The central anchor of the mole was created through floating an enormous vessel 104 m (114 yds.) in length,[7] and then sinking it at the appropriate place according to the plan for the mole. Obviously, on a sloping shore some portion of the original harbor locus would have been under water, the portion depending on the slope of the shore.

The question of whether it was necessary to dredge or to dig is important because of the difference in problems in developing the harbor. We will discuss later the difference in complexity between a digging and a dredging operation.

According to Testaguzza, the area of the harbor was about a third of a square mile and from 16.5 to 18 feet deep.[8] This would give the harbor's total water content as roughly 150,000,000 cubic feet. Our data suggest that the variable depth (16–18 feet) is caused by the variations in the bottom, not to different original heights of sand above sea level. We are thus in a quandary as to the degree of the total volume which is caused by different portions of the total excavation which are above sea level. For example, if the total area was originally already below the intended floor of the harbor, no sand would need to be moved; if all of the area were originally 16.5 feet above sea level, twice the volume of sand would have to be moved to get a 16.5 foot deep harbor. Since we are discussing a sloping shore, partly underwater in the original harbor area, partly an unknown amount above water level, we have assumed that the amount of sand needing removal averaged 16.5 feet in depth. With this assumption we believe that Testaguzza's figure for the volume of the harbor is a fair estimate of the volume of sand to be moved, that is about 150,000,000 cubic feet (see Chart 2).

In further analysis we relied heavily on data from the Goodchild and Forbes' article, "Roads and Land Travel."[9] We tentatively examined a number of different methods by which the task could have been done: by manpower, by ox-and-sledge, by donkey- mule- or ox-pannier. We do not have sufficient data to make informed judgments, but we believe that the direct manpower required by several of these methods will be about that for the Fucine Lake. We believe that the task could have been completed in from ten to twenty years. Less than ten, with some overcrowding of the work area; in more than ten if the work did not continue throughout the year (that is, if it was seasonal). (See appendix 4 for sample calculations.)

One of our approaches generally went as follows:

We have assumed that the soft alluvial soil involved would be pulled from the harbor area by ox teams using a pulled wooden scoop or sledge (Varro, *LL* 5.139).[10] We believe that under the circumstances a wheeled vehicle would have been impracticable in loose sand. We assume that each team would pull about one cubic foot of earth (160 pounds) per trip, and that the earth would have to be pulled an average of about 1,524 feet (one-fourth the width of the harbor—plus the same distance on the shore to deposit his load). Note that this assumption means that we always go, moving parallel to the sea, to the nearest edge from the center line; some sand will go all the way, including the dumping ground, the last bit will go but an inch. The ox team will return empty. (Refer to Appendix 4, Chart 3.) We assumed that as many as eight ox teams would work together, following each other continuously. Donald Sippel writes in detail on the difficulties of using an ox since it "belonging to the bovine family, is a cud-chewing animal and must have time each day to graze but time as well to complete the second stage of its digestive process." In addition, oxen are "also frequently bad-tempered, unpredictable, and dangerous, and if provoked, may attack their drivers." Sippel's study suggests that more oxen teams might be needed than a straight forward calculation would specify.[11]

We believe that the men needed for mole-building would have been but a minor fraction of the number engaged in sand-hauling; the individuals involved in mole-building, however, would have been much more highly skilled, in skills quite foreign to those required in other Roman city construction work.

We had less to go on when we evaluated the water-covered part of the task. We were unable to find an adequate evaluation of ancient dredging, although we found plenty of data suggesting that dredging was a familiar task in the period.[12] Our guess is that water dredging is somewhat more difficult than land digging, per cubic foot of sand moved. We do know that the Romans seemed to have had little trouble in digging canals, several of which were required in the harbor construction.

It should also be clear that we are uncertain as to the division between the land-based task and the water-borne one. Not only do we not know what percent of the original area from which the harbor was curved was under water, but we are not certain that, as land-based work went deeper, seepage from the ocean nearby did not change an originally land-based task into one plagued with a morass of mud, half land and half water and less desirable to work than either one. Our most useful insight into this problem from the ancient sources is Dio (40.11.4) who says that "first he [the builder of the Claudian harbor] excavated a not inconsiderable area of land; he built a retaining wall right around this excavated area and then let the sea come in."[13]

Analysis of the mole-building portion of the water-oriented task is less challenging. Mole-building was a well understood project in the ancient world. There was a minor innovation in the use of the enormous ship as the anchor piece of the key left mole; the use of hydraulic concrete was by the time well understood, but its use on a grand scale was less so.[14] The project was larger than most other harbor building projects but, since the depths were shallower, the site presented fewer construction complications. We can assume that the huge travertine building blocks (six to seven tons) forming the core of the mole were quarried from an accessible location (probably Tivoli) and transported by water to the point where they would be fitted to the final spot.

We believe that, all things considered, the harbor project was a slightly less difficult and less time-consuming one than the Fucine Lake effort. We believe that the man-hours required would have been fewer, and more important, perhaps, that the work was, on the average, at a significantly lower skill level. The mole-building and design was a task requiring a middle level of technology, lower than much of the tunnel work; the digging labor would need but a minor level of skill, less in total than that required in common farming.

We recognize that we differ from Meiggs in our assessment that the Ostian project was less difficult than was the Fucine one. He states in *Roman Ostia*, p. 54: "The building of a new harbour at Ostia was a considerably more difficult undertaking than the draining of the Fucine Lake, or the building of an aq-

HARBOR OF OSTIA

Sestertius of Nero (*BMC Emp.* 132 Pl. 41.7)

Obv.
Head of Nero

Legend:
NERO CLAVD CAESAR AVG GER PM
TRP P IMP PP

Rev.
View of Harbor of Ostia

Legend:
AVGVSTI POR OST

ueduct." We do not know the depth of the analysis on which Meiggs made his evaluation: we do know that we have accomplished a very thorough analysis of the Fucine one and as good an analysis of the Ostian one as can be made from data available.

From the viewpoint of our broader investigation into the manpower needs of the era, the deployment of labor into and out of this project would have been significantly less troublesome than the redeployment of the more sophisticated labor force involved in earlier analyses. At Ostia the force would have come from the farm: they would not have been exposed to an urban environment nor would they have had to learn any significant new skills; they would have easily returned to their traditional tasks.

A problem found in examining and in evaluating the Ostian project not encountered elsewhere was confusion as to the timing of the project. We are reasonably certain that the project commenced in A.D. 42. There is controversy, however, over the date of its completion.[15] One of the problems concerns a definition of what was meant by the "Port of Ostia." Certain parts were obviously finished earlier than others. Thus, an inscription tells us that a canal was finished in A.D. 46 which was hailed as an important completion.[16] The canal had a dual purpose: one, to provide vessel transit from the port to the city of Rome; the other, to reduce the danger of floods in the urban area. Apparently, the heralded completion was only of the flood control purpose; the only achievement mentioned in the inscription is that it "freed the city from the danger of inundation." By 62, we are sure that the harbor was in use by ships, for at that time Tacitus (*Ann.* 15.18.3) speaks of the loss of 200 ships within the moles. In addition, we know that in A.D. 64 the Emperor Nero issued a coin showing the completed harbor.[17] Had the project been completed much before A.D. 64, it is unlikely that Nero would have issued a coin advertising it. Most surely this would have been true had the completion been before A.D. 54, for before that time Nero would have been advertising a project completed solely by Claudius. An alternate explanation, offered by Meiggs, is that all the harbor was completed before Claudius died but that the coin merely marked the completion of the building program in the town and along the moles.[18] An examination of the coin involved does not particularly support that explanation; the thing most stressed on the coin is the shipping, the quays, and an imperial statue, one not recognizable as any individual ruler.

A suggestion sometimes made is that Nero's purpose in issuing the coin was to point up the value of the port in preventing a famine after the great fire of A.D. 64. Again, the payoff to Nero of such a symbolic coin is not apparent unless the port was finished after Nero's accession. The best guess as to the completion date is that it was sometime after Claudius' death but probably before A.D. 62. This would give a project completion time span from A.D. 42 to A.D. 62, or twenty years, substantially longer than the eleven years taken for the Fucine Lake.

MANPOWER CONCLUSIONS

The Harbor of Ostia project does not totally match the assumption of a homogeneous manpower pool which supports the rest of the study. Although the project is but 15 miles from Rome and is tightly bound into the metropolitan community, it is a different kind of task. A portion of the job (the earth moving task) is very similar to that common to farmers; the *conductores* involved may have directly recruited farmers to do the specific task; the farmers may have interchanged the Ostian task with their farm duties. Since the labor did not require special skills, it is possible that many different individuals were employed intermittently at the digging task. The primary skill in the digging phase would be, as we have visualized it, the ability to control a team of oxen, a skill, of course, but a widely held one.

The water-borne skills are just as specialized as brickmaking, carpentry, and pipe-fitting. However, since men with water-craft management skills and with skills in the water are rarely needed in city public building, they would have found little employment other than in the port construction. We suspect, indeed, that Claudius' managers imported many of these workmen for the special tasks, much as oilfield workers move from job to job worldwide today. If this was true, these workmen were recruited elsewhere, worked for a time in Ostia, and departed for some other water-based task elsewhere.

On the other hand, perhaps half of the labor on the port was engaged in standard everyday jobs of the kind continuously needed in any city. These workers were a part of the overall metropolitan labor pool, the group around which we are centering this study.

An important possibility as a source of a portion of the raw labor arises from the enormous manpower demands and the seasonal nature of the task of moving the very large quantity of grain from the ships in which it arrived at Ostia to the warehouses in which it was stored either at Rome or at Ostia. K. D. White emphasizes the immensity of the task:

> In the early Empire Rome's annual importation of grain from Egypt, Sicily and Africa involved what was by far the most massive handling operation known to the classical world, viz., off-loading from sea-going freighters . . . storing at the port of Ostia, and reloading into river barges for the final stage up the River around half a million tons of grain, in sacks weighing 28 kg (60 lb) apiece. This formidable operation will have required some 17 million sackloads, all carried on the backs of saccarii without any mechanical aids.[19]

Geoffrey Rickman, on the other hand, stresses the seasonality of the task: "That season [voyages for the corn supply] . . . stretched from late May to early September, or, at the outside from early March to early November."[20] It is obvious that there were available unemployed workers at Ostia for six to eight months a year; during this period the average annual lowest 24 hour temperature is 5 degrees C. (41 degrees F.) in January and in February the lowest temperature months.[21] These workers' main task was transporting sacks of grain weighing 60 lbs. apiece. Who would be better able to lift the sand from the harbor excavation? Perhaps their availability was an important factor in deciding to initiate the project—or at least to shift from ox-power to man-power for the hauling job. Sippel notes the difficulties besetting the lower classes in their search for work and includes as one of the possibilities for work the job of portering. "The difficulties of everyday life were further exacerbated by the limited opportunities for unskilled labor. Brickmaking, building construction and portering will practically exhaust the possibilities."[22]

We generalize, then, our evaluation of the Ostian project: It was a major user of labor and a part of the central Roman labor pool. Its impact on this pool was softened by the rather large number of peculiar specialties involved: some of them too rural for the city; some of them too maritime for an essentially inland city; some of them, also, may have been seasonally unemployed labor, normally employed in the ports' grain-hauling duty.

To relate the labor demands of the Ostian project to the broader ones of the Julio-Claudian base, the addition of the Harbor project would have made the Julio-Claudian peak from A.D.

42 until A.D. 50 more severe (see Chart 1 in Chapt. 2). After that date, and until A.D. 62, the work on the harbor would have helped the labor management problems by filling in a depression. One would like to say that the Ostian work concentrated the "water and farmer" work in the period to A.D. 50, and shifted to the supporting warehouses and cargo handling support phases after that. It is an attractive hypothesis, and seems to make sense, but our data are not sufficient to test its validity.

ENDNOTES TO CHAPTER VI

[1]See Meiggs for a discussion of the role of Puteoli in the food supply: *Roman Ostia,* 56–57.

[2]For a discussion of Roman ports see D. J. Blackmann, "Ancient Harbours in the Mediterranean," *IJNA* 11:2 (1982) 79–104 and 11:3 (1982), 185–211; he has an extensive bibliography, pp. 97–104.

[3]Meiggs, 591.

[4]O. Testaguzza, "The Port of Rome," *Archaeology* 17 (1964), 173–179.

[5]Both passages translated by Meiggs, 154.

[6]*Arch.,* 173.

[7]O. Testaguzza, *Portus* (Rome, 1970), 109.

[8]*Arch.,* 177.

[9]R. G. Goodchild and R. J. Forbes, *A History of Technology,* II (Oxford, 1956), 493–524.

[10]See K. D. White, *Greek and Roman Technology* (Ithaca, New York, 1984), 133.

[11]Donald Sippel, "Some Observations on the Means and Cost of the Transport of Bulk Commodities in the Late Republic and Early Empire," *AncW* 16 (1987), 36.

[12]White, *Greek and Rom. Tech.,* 109.

[13]Translation by Meiggs, 154.

[14]John P. Oleson, Robert L. Hohlfelder, Avner Raban, and Robert L. Vann, "The Caesarea Ancient Harbor Excavation Project," *Journal of Field Archaeology* 11 (1984), 285.

[15]Leonardo Dal Maso and Roberto Vighi, *Ostia-Port-Sacred Island* (Florence, 1975), 42; Meiggs, 161; 488.

[16]A photograph of the inscription appears in Testaguzza, *Portus,* 38.

[17]C. H. V. Sutherland, *Coinage in Roman Imperial Policy* (New York, 1951), 168.

[18]Meiggs, 56.

[19]*Greek and Roman Tech.,* 128.

[20]*The Corn Supply of Ancient Rome* (Oxford, 1980), 128.
[21]*World Climate* Chart provided by International Association for Medical Assistance to Travellers (1986).
[22]Sippel, "Dietary Deficiency," *AncW* 16 (1987), 50.

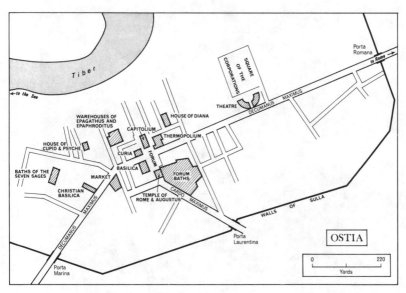

Map: Harbor of Ostia

The Claudian Connections. Painting by Zeno Diemer.
Confluent Aqua Anio and Aqua Claudia intersecting with the confluent Marcia, Tepula and Julia Aqueducts

VII. THE LATER JULIO-CLAUDIAN EMPERORS

Claudius and Nero were under less pressure to strengthen the imperium; Augustus and Tiberius had already developed a code of government, a feeling that an emperor was in accordance with tradition and had a legitimate right to govern. Thus, Claudius and Nero could spend less energy on strengthening political acceptance of the empire as an institution and could afford to provide vigorous support to riskier projects. The key difference between the demands on the later Julio-Claudians was that Claudius still had very high priority construction needs, essential to the society, while Nero's necessary projects were far less demanding. We will treat each of these last two in turn.

THE CLAUDIAN CONNECTIONS

Claudius' decisions were limited by his need to increase the food supply. The emperor came into power facing a near crisis; above all, he had to feed the people. Furthermore, he had to finish the aqueducts which Caligula had started; water for drink and for bathing was in the process of being provided, but needed finishing; he had to connect the water to the fountains of Rome. He did it. To do more would seem to be well nigh impossible.

Aqueducts require expensive manpower. Historically, there may have been doubts as to the ability of the government to take on manpower-hungry food projects as well. That Claudius could undertake the aqueduct completions, the lake drainage, and the port construction simultaneously without visible strain on either finances or manpower is strong corroborating evidence that Tiberius' long dry spell was self-generated; it was but five years since Tiberius had died. Claudius successfully made the connections: the water to the fountains, the drain to the lake, the pipeline to the food.

Of the three high priority projects, the one of lowest need would unquestionably have been the Fucine Lake. While its fertile soils were valuable, they were in the middle of the penin-

Aqua Claudia "arcus neroniani"

sula, at a distance from Rome with some rather steep moun-
tainous terrain on the road. The distance was but 53 miles, but
the path was hilly, and land transport can be expensive. Perhaps
Claudius accepted the added expense of the lake-draining only
because it fitted his overall scheme. The emperor possibly wanted
to provide full employment for laborers about to complete the
first phases of the nearby aqueduct program. Remember the
source of the aqueducts is but six miles from the Fucine Lake.
The laborers used in early phases of aqueduct building were
tunnel builders involved in taking the stream through ridges and
obstructions in the mountains on their way to the lower land
near the city. When the lower lands are reached, the nature of
the task changes from the task of tunnel drilling to that of arch
construction; the water level must be kept high above the lower
land so that the water can arrive in the city at an altitude sufficient
to provide water pressure for the city's distribution system. It
perhaps was more efficient to keep the tunnel builders employed
at their specialty in the draining of the Fucine Lake rather than
to retrain them into the much commoner arch building skill.

We have concluded that the draining of the Fucine Lake was
not a project performed by the city's labor force. As for the
aqueduct-building task, we suggested that the city crews picked
up the task where the tunnel digging stopped and the arch building began. The country crews built all the tunnels whether part
of the aqueduct or of the lake draining.

It is also possible that Claudius' aqueduct *conductores* were
fretting because, up in the colder hill country, they could not
keep their aqueduct force employed because of cold weather and
the problems inherent in the use of concrete in below freezing
temperatures. It is logical that the aqueduct builders could increase their total productivity by working in good weather on
the aqueducts, and when the temperature dropped, going down
into the tunnel where it would be acceptably warm. (Front. *Aq.*
2.123.)

We, therefore, suspect that the Fucine Lake project is an
example of a project undertaken to maintain an existing work
force and to increase total productivity at minimum marginal
cost.

We are impressed with Claudius. His decisions were logical:
he knew when to take a risk (the port); he integrated his decisions
(the lake and the aqueducts) and he knew that resources should
be expended for the good of his people. It is possible that Clau-

dius' team of talented civil servants, Pallas, Narcissus, and Callistus, were really responsible. Possibly. In that case we must add another credit; he knew how to select his factotums.

THE NERONIAN NIRVANA

Nero was but 16 years old when he began his reign in A.D. 54. Originally, he was *totally* dominated by his mother Agrippina.[1] His mother fell out of power about A.D. 55, losing out to a semi-regency under the control of Seneca and of Burrus which ended in A.D. 62. Thus, for the first eight years of his reign, Nero was not making the decisions. As might be expected under a regency, few important decisions were made, aside from constructing a house for the emperor (the Domus Transitoria). The sharp reduction in building programs starting at the end of the reign of Claudius and continuing into the regency should have created problems for the government; however, the port of Ostia was still being completed. If, as we believe, the digging and dredging work requiring non-urban laborers was completed shortly before A.D. 54, we can allocate some of the possibly redundant city labor of the period A.D. 54–62 to the work of constructing the warehouses and the harbor buildings. These would normally be the last to be built and would require standard urban construction workers. If so, it was not enough to prevent unrest in the city, for in A.D. 61 (Tac. *Ann*.14.42) and in A.D. 62 (Tac. *Ann*. 14.61.2) there was evidence of civil disturbances. Tacitus tells us that in A.D. 62, "A noisy crowd invaded the Palace. . . . she (the Emperor's wife, Poppaea) was now mad with fear of mass violence. . . ."[2] Yavetz says that economic stress was one of the main causes for riots.[3] We are tempted to suggest that the lay-off notices received by the work force upon the completion of the Harbor of Ostia triggered the riots which, in turn, persuaded Nero to commence his Gymnasium (see below).

When Nero finally gained full control in A.D. 62, he had but one major task of the triad required of the Julio-Claudians— "making merry." To provide means of entertainment for his people, he built the Gymnasium of Nero in A.D. 62; the baths of Nero in A.D. 64; an amphitheater in A.D. 65; and rebuilt the Circus Maximus in A.D. 65.

The period from A.D. 64 on must be viewed in a different light, for the great fire occurred in that year. The fire happened providentially at a time and in a place which would have delighted the heart of a modern slum clearer. Right in the center of Rome a maze of older buildings (plus the Emperor's old palace) was completely destroyed. Nero responded nobly, rebuilding the devastated areas to top quality against high quality new zoning rules (including a new house for himself—the Domus Aurea, one of the wonders of the era).

Our general evaluation of the building programs of Nero is that they were logical, reasonably well timed, and responsive to what seemed to be the paramount needs of the city at the time. The city's highest priority needs had been met through the vigorous efforts of Claudius.

There is evidence that Nero had financial troubles; toward the end of his reign he reduced the precious metal content of the coinage, an action which has earned him a bad press from numismatists,[4] but which did not seem to bother the general Roman population or modern economists. To an economist, the sudden dumping of Tiberius' hoard from his treasury into the economy through Caligula's building program should have done more to cause inflation than all of Nero's coin clipping. Braudel summarizes the arguments suggesting that a non-policy influx of precious metals can have an inflationary influence on price levels.[5] Unfortunately, our evidence of price changes is almost nonexistent except long-term.

THE NERONIAN NEMESIS

Nero has not been treated kindly by historians, beginning with the extremely biased ancient sources. Pliny, for example, judged building programs on unacceptable grounds; he criticized Nero's attempt to cut a canal across the Isthmus of Corinth because the constructions were undertaken in spite of unfavorable omens. As an indication of the validity of the omens the author states that others (King Demetrius, Caesar the Dictator, and Gaius) who had attempted such an undertaking, died prematurely (*NH* 4.10). Consequently, Charles H. Herkert states:

> This is the most important feature of Pliny as an historian, he allows his prejudices to color his interpretations . . . The most notable example of this are Nero and Vespasian. Everything that Nero does is put in an unfavorable light. . . . On the other hand, Vespasian can do no wrong.[6]

Pliny, a writer during Vespasian's reign, is merely catering to the wishes of the emperor who was very vindictive against Nero, his overthrown predecessor.[7]

Next, let us look at how Tacitus, Suetonius and Dio report the great fire of A.D. 64:

Tac. Ann. 15.38.1	*Suet. Nero 38.1*	*Dio 62.15.1–2*
Disaster followed. Whether it was *accidental* or *caused* by the emperor's criminal act is uncertain—both versions have supporters . . .[8]	For under cover of displeasure at the ugliness of the old buildings and the narrow, crooked streets, he *set fire to the city* so *openly* . . . Viewing the conflagration from the tower of Maecenas and exulting, as he said in "the beauty of the flames," he sang the whole of the "Sack of Ilium," in his regular stage costume.[9]	After this Nero set his heart on accomplishing what had doubtless always been his desire, namely to make an end to the whole city and realm during his lifetime . . . Accordingly he *secretly . . . caused* them (his men) at first *to set fire* to one or two or even several buildings in different parts of the city . . .[10]
Sequitur clades (sc. incendium), *forte an dolo principis incertum* (nam utrumque auctores prodidere . . .	Nam quasi offensus deformitate veterum aedificiorum et angustiis flexurisque vicorum, *incendit urbem* tam *palam* . . . Hoc incendium e turre Maecenatiana prospectans laetusque "flammae," ut aiebat, "pulchritudine" Halosin Ilii in illo suo scaenico habitu decantavit.	

Of these writers two state flatly that Nero started the fire: only Tacitus hedges his account by saying that the fire might have been accidental. Today, modern historians believe that it is unlikely that Nero could have started the fire.[11]

The Christian Church added its voice to those of the biased ancient sources. The Church hated Nero, too. To it he was the Anti-Christ; to it his burnings of the Christians led to the fall of Rome. We see this view of him in the writings of the Church Fathers (Tertullian, *Apol.* 5; Lactantius, *De Mortibus Persecutorum* 2; St. Augustine, *Civitas Dei* 20.19).[12]

There were those, however, even in ancient times who held the opposite view, as Josephus notes:

> For many historians have written the story of Nero, of whom some, because they were well treated by him, have out of gratitude been careless of truth, while others from hatred and enmity towards him have so shamelessly and recklessly revelled in falsehoods as to merit censure. Nor can I be surprised at those who have lied about Nero, since even when writing about his predecessors they have not kept to the facts of history. Surely they had no hatred for those emperors, since they lived long after them.[13]

Nevertheless, although a pro-Neronian tradition must have existed, we get surprisingly few indications of it today. As Momigliano remarks, "Our information is consequently one sided; we do not know the name of even one of those favorable historians whose existence Josephus attests."[14] On the other hand, even in our unfavorable ancient sources, we can find a few comments favorable to Nero. Among these passages would be those referring to the "second coming" of Nero (Tac. *Hist.* 2.8; *Ann.* 4.5; *Hist.* 1.10; Zonaras 11.18; John of Antioch, fr. 104 [Mueller, *FHG,* Vol. 4]; Suet. *Nero* 57). One Suetonian passage (*Otho* 7.1) tells of Otho, now called Nero, with his approval, by the common people, setting up Nero's bust and statues. In another passage in Suetonius, Vitellius applauded the songs of Nero as he made funerary offerings to him (Suet. *Vit.* 11.2). In a third passage Suetonius (*Nero* 57.1) says:

> . . . yet there were some who for a long time decorated his tomb with spring and summer flowers, and now produced his statues on the rostra in the fringed toga, and now his edicts, as if he were still alive. . . .[15]

Perhaps the most influential of the evaluations is the following summary of Nero's reign by the Emperor Trajan as recorded by Sex. Aurelius Victor, *Liber de Caesaribus* 5. 1–2. This has been translated by J.G.C. Anderson thus:

> Having ruled, as a mere youth [adolescens], for as many years as his stepfather, nevertheless, i.e. in spite of his youth, for five years [quinquennium] he was so effective, especially in improving the city, that Trajan with justice often declared that all other emperors fell behind Nero's five years [Neronis quinquennio]; during that period he also (i.e. besides improving the city) reduced Pontus to the status of a province by leave of Polemon, after whom it is called Pontus Polemoniacus, and likewise the Cottian Alps on the death of King Cottius.[16]

Additional information on "improving the City" is provided by Victor's epitomator. He states: "He built an amphitheater and baths in the city."

The passage has problems. It seems to say that Nero did well while a youth, but did poorly afterwards. The first problem is that the events described as evidence of good rule did not take place during his first five years: an apparent quandary. However, it is resolved when we recognize that in Latin a man is an "adolescens" until he is thirty years old (Cic. *Tusc*.2.1.2), thus permitting Nero's good years to be any time during his reign.[17]

A thumbnail description of Nero's accomplishments is given by Martial: "What is worse than Nero? What is better than his baths?" (7.34.4).

We believe Nero to have been a successful and vigorous builder, who did an excellent job of meeting the city's needs rationally and logically.

Nero's nemesis, then, is to go down in history as the Anti-Christ, the man who fiddled while Rome burned.

Most scholars accept the conventional interpretation of Trajan's remark, namely, that Nero's reign was outstanding before his assuming full control sometime after five years.[18] In other words, it was good while Seneca and Burrus were in control. The attribution of Nero's good quinquennium to the first five years of his reign has concerned many scholars.[19] The ancient literary source in question (Aurelius Victor, *De Caesaribus* 5.1–2 and his Epitomator) contains serious anachronisms if the whole citation is considered. More seriously, there are no believable accomplishments (other than the completion of Claudius' harbor) which would support a positive accomplishment record for Nero's first quinquennium. We cannot accept the encomium received for Nero's first five years nor the consequent praise given to Nero's early factotums, Seneca and Burrus.

ENDNOTES TO CHAPTER VII

[1]We see on the coins the main evidence for a belief in Agrippina's influence during Nero's reign. *BMC Emp*. I, pl. 38, nos. 1–6.

[2]Trans. by Michael Grant, *Annals* (Baltimore, Md.), 331.

[3]*Plebs and Princeps*, 26.

[4]Harold Mattingly, *Roman Coins* (London, 1967), 122–123.

[5]Fernand Braudel, *The Mediterranean* (New York, 1949), I, 517–523.

[6]"Historical Commentary Drawn from the Natural History of Pliny the Elder for Years 54–76 A.D." (unpublished Ph.D. dissertation, University of Pennsylvania, 1956), 4.

[7]M.P. Charlesworth, "Flaviana," *JRS* 27 (1937), 55.

[8]Trans. by Grant, *Annals,* 351.

[9]Loeb Classical Library, trans. by J.C. Rolfe, 155.

[10]Dio's *Roman History,* VIII, trans. by E. Cary, Loeb Classical Library (London, 1925), 111.

[11]Michael Grant, *Nero* (New York, 1970), 170; A. Momigliano, "Nero," *CAH* X, 722–723.

[12]For further discussion see article by Joseph Plescia, "The Persecution of the Christians in the Roman Empire," *Latomus* 30 (1971), 128.

[13]Josephus, *Jewish Antiquities,* IX, trans. by Louis H. Feldman, Loeb Classical Library (Cambridge, Mass., 1945), 473, 475; 20.154–155.

[14]*CAH* X (1934), 702.

[15]*Nero,* trans. by J.C. Rolfe, Loeb Classical Library (1965), 185.

[16]"Trajan on the *Quinquennium* Neronis," *JRS* 1 (1911), 176.

[17]See M.K. Thornton, "The Enigma of Nero's Quinquennium," *Historia* 22 (1973), 570–582; J.G.F. Hind, "Is Nero's Quinquennium an Enigma?", *Historia* 24 (1975), 629–630.

[18]R. Syme, *Emperors and Biography* (Oxford, 1971), 106–110.

[19]Here is a list of many scholars who have written on the Quinquennium: J. G. C. Anderson, "Trajan on the Quinquennium Neronis," *JRS* 1 (1911), 173–179, with note by F. Haverfield, 178–179; P. Faider, *Études sur Sénèque* (Ghent, 1921); M. A. Levi, *Nerone e i suoi Tempi* (Milan, 1949); I. Lana, *Lucio Annaeo Seneca* (Turin, 1955); F. A. Lepper, "Some Reflections on the Quinquennium Neronis," *JRS* 47 (1957), 95–103; R. Syme, *Tacitus* (Oxford, 1958); O. Murray, "The Quinquennium Neronis and the Stoics," *Historia* 14 (1965), 41–61; G. W. Bowersock, "Suetonius and Trajan," *Hommages à M. Renard,* I, ed. J. Bibauw (Bruxelles, 1969), 119ff.; J. G. F. Hind, "The Middle Years of Nero's Reign," *Historia,* 20 (1971), 488–505; R. Syme, *Emperors and Biography* (Oxford, 1971); E. Cizek, *L Époque de Néron et les controverses idéologiques* (Leiden, 1972); M. K. Thornton, "The Enigma of Nero's Quinquennium," *Historia* 22 (1973), 570–582; Hind, "Is Nero's Quinquennium an Enigma?" *Historia* 24 (1975), 629–630; B. M. Levick, *Studies in Latin Literature and Roman History,* III., ed. by C. Deroux, *Collection Latomus* CL XXX (1983), 211–225.

VIII. IMPLICATIONS AND CONCLUSIONS

While we originally intended our research to be an archaeological study of public works program, it very soon became a much wider study of the political and the economic conditions which surround the decisions to build; this, in turn, led us to an examination of the individual emperor's methods for controlling and for managing public expenditures. The five emperors who were the dynasty practiced very different management styles; thus, our chronological analysis of their performance in a key public sector gave us an unexpectedly rewarding opportunity for comparative evaluation of both the emperors and their management styles. Much of what we say in the following paragraphs came from the resulting insights.

THE MULTIPLIER

But first we need to defend our assumption that the public building programs are significant enough to a non-modern society to make an important impact on that society's general welfare. That assumption is subject to challenge from those who say that, after all, public works were at best but a modest bit of the Roman economy; to put too much emphasis on their cyclical nature is to exaggerate their importance to the Roman citizen's every-day living. After all, private building was going on at a great pace throughout the Julio-Claudian period, and you are completely ignoring that much larger segment for your study of the more visible temples, baths, and fountains.

This line of argument is, of course, immediately subject to attack because it is obvious that, in Rome's case, the workmen who were required to do the public building had to come from somewhere, and had to be fed and to be sheltered in Rome while they were employed in public works. What is missed, however, is that the people engaged in feeding and in sheltering the direct laborers will themselves need support, and will from their own production rewards be anxious to consume more of the good things in life. Modern day economists have spent much time in trying to quantify the amount that an economy will change for

103

every increment of autonomous investment (e.g., public works programs) that is injected into an economy. Their conclusion, defended by logic that is independent of the time or circumstances, is that the result will be expansion of that economy by a factor, known as the multiplier, which is dependent on the consumption habits of the specific society. The originator of the concept of the multiplier is J. M. Keynes. His figure for a typical modern community was 5 for the multiplier: for every unit of autonomous investment injected into an economy the economy will grow by 5 times as much.[1] For different economies, the factor will be different but will depend on the degree to which the economy in question consumes all that it produces at once rather than uses it to enhance future consumption (building an aqueduct is an example of using today's production to enhance future production). We cannot calculate this for the Roman economy for lack of data. If the data were available, we could calculate the multiplier. As a matter of information, the greater the degree to which an economy immediately consumes all that it produces, the greater the size of the multiplier. In the Roman economy we can only speculate, but generally a very poor economy cannot afford to save, it must eat or starve. Rome was a wealthy economy, but far less so than Britain or the U.S. in the 20th century. One would speculate that the Roman multiplier was considerably larger than the modern figure, therefore, more potent in its influence.[2] Keynes himself uses an ancient economy as a reference when he talks of the boon which pyramid-building was to the Egyptian society. As Keynes said:

> Ancient Egypt was doubly fortunate, and doubtless owed to this its fabled wealth, in that it possessed *two* activities, namely pyramid-building as well as the search for the precious metals, the fruits of which since they could not serve the needs of man by being consumed did not stale with abundance.[3]

BUILDING MANAGEMENT SYSTEMS

Now to return to the insights gained from this study. Augustus was in an unusual position because he was operating in an era of comparatively rapid change; the revolution had created a need for new and potentially stable institutions. He could innovate against a weakened conservative opposition.

Augustus enhanced his control of Rome's building programs, first, by reorganizing its management structure and, second, by shifting its financial supervision. We will discuss each of these in turn.

Reorganizing the Management Structure

During the Republic the officials responsible both for the maintenance of existing public works and for the initiation of new building programs were the censors. Their appointment was for five years, but they actually served only for 18 months of the five years, leaving the task unsupervised for 42 months out of each five–year interval. The censors, as Strong notes, were "amateur without a professional staff of advisors, and they were often at the mercy of unreliable contractors."[4] These officials (ex-consuls) had already made their reputation elsewhere and would normally not be ambitious. Not a recipe for assured quality performance nor one for getting professional advice as to needs and priorities. Augustus' innovation was the replacement of the censor with an aedile, a lower ranking position. Since the office of aedile required continuous service, its occupant could envision a program which provided him with an opportunity for personal advancement. Much Augustan building required planning and time for completion of the work. The disadvantage of using a lower ranking official was, of course, the risk of his not possessing sufficient personal status to get the ear of senior decision makers. Augustus overcame this disadvantage by putting in Agrippa as aedile and by supporting his every effort. It was a drastic step; Agrippa had already been a victorious general, a praetor and a consul. Augustus' innovation worked. Agrippa created a permanent staff of specialists who supervised the future water needs of Rome. Augustus' solution needed, of course, an unusual man to take over the task, one who was intensely loyal and competent and was willing to take what was considered to be a demotion.

Perhaps the more subtle aspect of Augustus' action here was the degree to which his reorganization reduced the ability of the senators themselves to get involved in the day-to-day decisions; a strong aedile would do all that he could to make the job his own, not that of every amateur in town! Senatorial powers and imperial powers were still in a state of flux; Augustus' long term political objective was the emasculation of the Senate. Despots may not be democratic, but they make the aqueducts run on time!

Shifting the Financial Supervision

Next, Augustus took advantage of a long standing custom of the Roman nobility. As Strong states, "It became established custom for a *vir triumphalis* to use part of the booty to erect a commemorative building—a *monumentum deorum immortalium* or an *ornamentum urbis*" (Cic. *De Lege Agraria* 2.61).[5] Taking advantage of this custom, Augustus paid personally for much of his building program. Thus, for the key portions of that program, he had removed the necessity of obtaining the Senate's approval; he could do what he wanted to do without asking anyone. He only asked Senatorial approval for small constructions such as the repair of the shrines (*RG* 4.17). By asking the Senate for permission for some building, Augustus made it less obvious that he was bypassing the traditional governing body and was disrupting the *mos maiorum*. He got more and more control into his own Imperial hands. A secondary effect, perhaps of greater importance to Augustus, was that through this device the credit for what were frequently very popular programs went to him personally.

The traditional way by which the Senate had controlled strong men was to cut off their money supply as Pompey found out when he requested money from the Senate to pay his troops (Dio 37, 49-50.1; Suet. *Caes.* 19). When Augustus destroyed the differences between the Emperor's personal wealth and the wealth of the State, he enhanced his power enormously. His personal wealth was the product of the success of the Roman armies; the booty was as much the State's as the Emperor's, at least in theory, even if it was not as certainly so in the *mos maiorum*. According to Strong, "In the last two centuries of the Republic this [*manubiae*: the commander's share of booty] was often an enormous figure."[6] Augustus used his *manubiae* in the service of the state; it was not misappropriation of funds, but it was an exceedingly successful power play.

Augustus' actions in seizing control of visible building programs and of funding systems were not surprising. Strong men of many countries and in many eras have done likewise. Nor were his methods particularly innovative. Much earlier Sulla had used long-term *curatores* of public works to control building; Augustus' use of his *manubiae* was in accordance with long standing custom. It is unusual that Augustus managed to keep control of the building officials and of the means of financing buildings and to pass on this ability to his successors. Obviously

Augustus' methods were successful in meeting his needs, but one man's new deal tends to lose its potency as rulers change. Augustus' good fortune came from the length of his rule: He gained the imperium in 27 B.C.; he remained in full control until his death in A.D. 14, a period of 41 years! By the time a new man took over, Augustus' innovations had become Rome's unwritten constitution—a new *mos maiorum*. His successor, Tiberius, was by nature a cautious man but, in his view, Augustus' innovations had been transformed by time into the conservative way and had become the custom of the ancestors. Augustus' innovations were totally successful: power over public construction had been transferred for a long time to come. Claudius formalized the actual transfer when he changed the words by which the maintenance boards operated from *ex decreto senatus* to *ex auctoritate Caesaris* (*CIL* 6.9034).

FACTOTUMS

Our definition of a factotum differs slightly from the dictionary's. The dictionary says that a factotum is a person having diverse activities or responsibilities; that is, a general servant. Our factotum will have diverse responsibilities and he will be a *public* servant. He may be an individual or a member of a small group of factotums who form a personal "kitchen cabinet" to the emperor.[7] They will perform both advisory and executive duties and may be in direct charge of particular programs of great personal importance to the emperor.

In our definition, the operating sphere of such an aide may be broad or less broad but must be in areas of high importance to the realm. He need not occupy a formal position in the government; he may incidentally be a Secretary of State, a Chancellor of the Exchequer, a Chief of Staff, or a Commander of the Imperial Guard, but those titles do not necessarily make a factotum nor does the absence of a title prevent him from being one. Absolute trust and delegated power in critical areas are the essence. Note that with the word "factotum" we are attempting to introduce into the general lexicon a carefully defined word to identify a widely occurring phenomenon for which we believe there is no alternative word.

No Roman emperor could hope to perform all key administrative tasks; he needed a factotum to provide ideas, to serve as a sounding board, to reconcile opposing ideas or factions, sometimes to carry out a particularly important task. The ruler's selection of a factotum was an extremely important decision. In many cases, the emperor's selection of his principal advisors would change the whole performance of the regime for better or for worse. Many rulers have used factotums over the years: Napoleon had his Talleyrand; Henry II, his Beckett; Roosevelt, his Harry Hopkins; William I, his Bismarck; and Woodrow Wilson, his wife and Colonel House. So it was in the case of the Julio-Claudians. In their choice of factotums, as we will show, two Julio-Claudians were successful; two, unsuccessful. What are the underlying requirements and constraints which determine whether a particular choice would be a good one?

Factotums, in the sense used here, differ in an important way from that of "client," a term with a substantial place in the literature on the empire, but the difference is in the viewpoint rather than in the relationship itself.[8] A client supports a patron; the patron supports the client. But the principal flow of value is from the patron to the client; on a net basis the patron gives and the client takes. A factotum, in the definition intended here, gives, and his patron takes. A factotum is badly needed; his chief would be much the worse off were he inadequate. This arises automatically from our definition that the factotum works in areas of high importance to the realm. Indeed, one of our theses is that the factotum *makes* the patron, to some extent.

Their power comes because they have the trust of their chief; loyalty to him is an absolute necessity. Augustus' factotums included Agrippa and Maecenas; Claudius', Pallas and Narcissus; Nero's, Seneca and Burrus; Tiberius', Sejanus. Their competences, or lack of them, we believe, were important contributing factors to the success or failure of their chiefs. Their names came up again and again in our research on building programs. Frequently they were behind-the-scenes managers of key programs.

Paul Pigors states:

> There is abundant historical evidence that despots and dictators are very partial to the free emergence of talent from obscurity so long as the aspirant for power is willing to place himself unreservedly at the disposal of the master . . . In fact, all dictators have tried to stabilize their power by developing a class of able functionaries whose entire fortune rests on the successful maintenance of their regime.[9]

Our analysis of the Julio-Claudian factotums deepens our understanding of the accomplishments of their chiefs, the Em-

perors. Let us start with a statement of their two basic requirements: they must be, first, intellectually competent and second,
absolutely loyal persons incapable of being subverted either by
ambition, by class, by ideology or by tradition. The most dangerous factotum to an emperor is one who aspires to the emperor's power as we shall see in the case of Sejanus.

AUGUSTUS

Augustus chose a dangerous factotum. By the time of Augustus' accession, Agrippa was already a famous man. He had
insured his patron's accession by able leadership of Augustan
forces against Sextus Pompeius (Suet. *Aug*. 16.2)[10] and against
Antony (Dio 51.21.3).[11] He performed his duties as aedile so
effectively that they contributed greatly to Augustus' cause, an
accomplishment that enhanced his own political standing as well
(Dio 49.43.1; Pliny, *NH* 36.104; Front. *Aq*. 9).[12] Why then was
Agrippa willing to serve Augustus as a factotum when he had
the accomplishments to be a Roman leader in his own right?
Why would Augustus have him? Such men are dangerous! The
evidence is clear that Augustus was aware of the risk of trusting
Agrippa. Augustus and Agrippa had been schoolmates at Apol-
lonia (Vell. 2.59.5),[13] but that did not insure loyalty; another
schoolmate, also later one of Augustus' generals (Salvidienus
Rufus), attempted to sell out to Antony and was put to death by
Augustus (Suet. *Aug*. 66.2; Appian, *BC*. 5.66.278; Dio 48.33.3;
Livy, *Per*. 127).

The emperor did everything in his power to bind Agrippa
to the regime, to make the success of Augustus and the success
of his factotum be the same thing. He gave him the *proconsulare
imperium* as well as a share in the *tribunicia potestas* (Dio
54.12.4).[14] Augustus, on what he thought was his own death bed,
indicated that Agrippa was to be his successor by giving him his
signet ring (Dio 53.31.2-4).[15] He gave him to wife first his niece,
then his daughter Julia, to insure that Agrippa's descendants at
least would be of the Julio-Claudian dynasty. According to Dio
(54.6.5), Maecenas said that, "Augustus has made Agrippa so
great that he will now have to make him his son-in-law or put
him to death." We do not know whether Agrippa was by nature
a very loyal person or whether he appreciated the careful management of his career by Augustus; in any case, Agrippa showed
unswerving loyalty towards Augustus.

Forum of Augustus, Rome

Agrippa had but one drawback—his humble origin (Vell. 2.127.1; cf. Suet. *Gaius* 23.1). Reinhold states that Agrippa's suppression of his nomen "Vipsanius" "is supported by all inscriptions, . . . in which he is always called M. Agrippa or simply Agrippa."[16] The Vipsanius family is mentioned only in connection with Agrippa.[17] With his military accomplishments and his friend-of-the-people reputation, he might very likely have overcome his obscure background. Possibly his loyalty was a result of his knowledge of the somewhat checkered careers of his *novus homo* predecessors, Marius and Cicero.[18] Wiseman notes: "For most *novi,* the only road to such tangible indexes of success as priesthoods and consulship was by hard work, servility, or luck— and frequently a combination of all three."[19]

Augustus' reasons for taking a chance are easy to see. Agrippa did almost everything superlatively: aqueduct building, political dealing, military command, detailed organizational development.

Augustus had a second factotum, Maecenas, also not of senatorial ancestry. We do not discuss his career because his skills were not applied to projects of the kind we are discussing.

Augustus had another man to whom he went after the death of Agrippa. However, this man also served as Augustus' last chance to carry on the dynasty. This was Tiberius, brought forth as the heir after a series of deaths which nearly eliminated the Julio-Claudian succession. Agrippa's death in 12 B.C. at the age of fifty-one was unexpected; he left a program of aqueduct building and repair that was of the highest priority. At Agrippa's death, according to Dio (54.31.2): "Augustus felt the need of an assistant in the public business, one who would far surpass all the others in both rank and influence, so that he might transact all business promptly and without being the object of envy and intrigue. Therefore, he reluctantly chose Tiberius." In this way, Tiberius became Augustus' factotum with the task of finishing the Agrippa-planned programs; by 4 B.C. Agrippa's programs were completed. Tiberius, however, did not supervise these programs for their final two years because he was sulking in Rhodes. Tiberius returned to Rome in A.D. 2. As Barbara Levick says: "His [Tiberius'] influence on Augustus' actions could be detected not long after . . . since A.D. 4 his influence had been paramount and hardly challengable."[20] (Jerome Carcopino believes that Tiberius did not finish all of Agrippa's projects; he believes that initial steps to build the Harbor of Ostia were underway when

Agrippa died, and were then abandoned.)[21] Augustus' building record is in two unlike parts. Projects initiated before 4 B.C. are heavy, necessary, and vigorously pursued. Those after 4 B.C. are desultory, of low importance and concentrated on restorations and rebuilding projects. (See Chart 1 in Chapt. 2.)

In 14 A.D. Tiberius became Emperor. The building programs from A.D. 14 until Tiberius' death in A.D. 37 are of exactly the same caliber as those from A.D. 4 until A.D. 14. (See Endnote 2, Chapter 4.)

It is hard not to make the connections. It was not the emperor who caused the impressive building programs of the early Augustan regime—it was his factotum Agrippa. It was not the idea of Augustus to collapse the program during the last half of the reign, it was that of his factotum Tiberius. The only thing that changed was the factotum. And the non-building factotum became the non-building emperor.

TIBERIUS

Tiberius seems to have employed but one factotum, but that one was a near disaster. In general, Tiberius was a "do-nothing" emperor, so his need for building specialists was nearly zero. He seems to have delegated his military and diplomatic work through normal channels until, half way through his reign, in A.D. 26 Tiberius moved to Capri and governed from there. Tacitus (*Ann.* 4.57) states that he was persuaded by Sejanus to move. Sejanus, according to Tacitus (*Ann.* 4.41), persuaded the emperior to move so that Sejanus would gain the following advantages:

> Access to the emperor would be under his own [Sejanus'] control, and letters, for the most part being conveyed by soldiers, would pass through his hands. Caesar too, who was already in the decline of life, would soon, when enervated by retirement, more readily transfer to him the functions of empire; envy towards himself would be lessened when there was an end to his crowded levees and the reality of power would be increased by the removal of its empty show.[22]

In fact, such a move required the creation of a factotum to serve in the city and Sejanus acquired additional functions to add to those he already possessed. Sejanus was already sole commander of the Praetorian Guard, a potentially threatening position. Sejanus, an equestrian, had shown considerable competence, and had been of use to Tiberius in solving other political problems successfully. Perhaps Tiberius thought Sejanus' being in the equestrian order prevented him from aspiring to be princeps, but shortly after giving Sejanus the highest position he could give him, Tiberius changed his mind and in A.D. 31 had Sejanus put to death. Tiberius claimed in his letter denouncing Sejanus that he (Tiberius) could no longer trust the Prefect of the Praetorian Guard (Dio 58.9.2-6). Interestingly enough, Tiberius' largest new building project (other than his private palace) was, at Sejanus' suggestion, to build new barracks for the Praetorian Guard, thus moving the force inside the city. An emperor who permitted such a step would be extremely nervous about the loyalty of the guards' commander (Sejanus), regardless of his social order. Indeed, Suetonius says that at the time of denouncement of Sejanus, Tiberius, waiting in Capri, had ships ready to carry him (Tiberius) away if a coup should be attempted (*Tib.* 65.2).

It was Macro who was behind the scenes carrying out Tiberius' instructions to get rid of Sejanus. He was rewarded with Sejanus' former command—and became the man who saw to it that Tiberius was finally smothered to death (Tac. *Ann.* 6.50). Never trust a military man with too much power!

Sejanus was not involved in building programs; his history, however, makes clear the risks an emperor faces when he selects his factotums, and clarifies the strategies adopted later on by a far more successful builder, Claudius. The only safe factotum is one with no chance whatsoever to turn his coat. An ex-slave makes a fine possibility.

CALIGULA (GAIUS)

Our evidence for Caligula's management systems is scant: Tacitus' account is lost; Suetonius spends most of his narrative in telling lurid tales of the debauchery of the regime but he does tell us that he "began an aqueduct in the region near Tivoli" (*Calig.* 21); Frontinus confirms this by writing that he began two aqueducts (Anio Novus and Claudia) in the second year of his reign (*Aq.* 1.13).

He seems to have treated his supporters cruelly: He put to death (Philo, *Leg.* 41–161) Macro, who had insured his succession (Tac. *Ann.* 6.50). Those senators who were responsible for convening the Senate were too frightened to do so. They feared Caligula would think the act of convening would be a sign of incipient insubordination (Dio 59.2.1). Not an environment which would create factotums! Note, however, the possible role of Callistus discussed below. Thus, Caligula managed his affairs alone.

We are not happy with the idea that after Macro's death, Caligula operated without the services of a factotum. From a building viewpoint, Caligula ranks high among the emperors; his most impressive contribution is the inception of the two aqueducts, the Claudia and the Anio Novus, but he does a major expansion of the Domus Tiberiana also. The discussions of Caligula's reign by Suetonius and Dio do not suggest that his interests would have been very deeply involved in personal administration of building programs even though these projects were of a high priority in a growing city. He had to have a manager and a factotum. Dio gives us some clues, but they are at a lower level of confidence than we have had in other reigns. Since Dio's interest is not managerially oriented, he would be unlikely to identify powerful and successful managers in the realm unless incidentally. Fortunately, he does just that. Three times Callistus is mentioned in a context which suggests that he had high influence with Caligula (Dio 59.19.6; 59.25.7; 59.29.1). Callistus later is a factotum to Claudius who completed the aqueducts. Thus, it is a reasonable hypothesis that Callistus was a factotum of Caligula; we are certain that Callistus was carried over into Claudius' reign. Callistus was a freedman; his suitability as a factotum is discussed under Claudius, later in this study. If our hypothesis is valid, then Caligula was well supplied with a highly competent factotum—not, however, necessarily loyal. Dio (59.29.1) states:

> As he continued to play the madman in every way, a plot was formed against him [Caligula] by Cassius Chaerea and Cornelius Sabinus, though they were tribunes in the praetorian guard. There were a good many, of course, in the conspiracy and privy to what was being done, among them Callistus and the prefect [of the praetorian guard], practically all his courtiers were won over both on their own account and for the common good. And those who did not take part in the conspiracy did not reveal it when they knew of it, and were glad to see a plot formed against him.[23]

We include Dio's statement because it is part of our hypothesis that a freedman is a good factotum because he can be trusted. In this case, Callistus was part of a plot; thus, a freedman who could not be trusted. In this case, however, while he was a member of a broadly spread plot, he was not an instigator.

We feel very uncomfortable in presuming that Caligula was

a successful emperor given the horror stories that Suetonius and Dio wrote concerning his reign. However, we do not have Tacitus' account for the reign of Caligula. Since Tacitus generally tones down the melodramatic flamboyance of Suetonius and Dio, perhaps even in our literary sources Caligula would appear in a different light if we had the Tacitean account.

We can use the imperial building program as a significant indicator of the overall success of an emperor's reign since no other overall measure of an emperor's performance exists. Our literary sources are of high importance, particularly where they are written nearly contemporaneously with the events they describe. There are, however, serious risks inherent in depending too closely on their description of events and on the analyses they make. With the Julio-Claudian literary sources we need to be particularly cautious. While Suetonius and Tacitus are nearly contemporaneous to Augustus and the Julio-Claudians, they can be suspected of writing as if change from the old *mos maiorum* was always a mistake (Suet. *Calig.* 22), and as if parsimony (Suet. *Calig.* 37), private morality (Tac. *Ann.* 16.21), and ascetic living (Tac. *Ann.* 3.55) were essential to good government and as if any event of the day was unfavorable if it did not conform to some mythical golden era (Tac. *Ann.* 1.7).

Our historians are of the Senatorial class or use Senatorial records as their sources. They strongly disapprove of the subordination of the Senate and of the aggrandizement of the Emperor. If Charles II had written a biography of Cromwell, would professional historians have trusted it? Under such conditions the scholar must search out alternate sources for evaluation and must develop supporting standards for judging performance. Our use of building programs as an indicator of imperial competence has its own disadvantages: it lacks richness of content and overemphasizes the economic and managerial skills at the expense of the more human values. Nevertheless, it measures in an orderly and comprehensive way something not covered by the literary sources. Above all, the evidence from the building programs is totally neutral since it is derived from archaeological remains and from technical literature. We do not claim this evidence as the predominant evaluative tool; it cannot replace literary sources but it can furnish one type of evidence to counterbalance a bias that can easily exist in any literary source.

Given this dilemma we must either presume that our measure of building programs as evidence of general managerial competence is unreliable or that Suetonius and Dio with a strongly conservative bias have grossly maligned Caligula. In the loom of history the lurid stories have little meaning; Caligula was personally corrupt if the details were true. But Rome seemed to have proceeded quite satisfactorily through his reign. If the second hypothesis that Caligula was maligned is true, then our research has provided a significant contribution to history: Caligula's portrayal as shown in ancient sources is tainted.

We can present one other possibility of reconciling Caligula's strong building programs with his unimpressive reputation from the literary sources. We argue that by the time of Caligula the bureaucracy was so established by the previous actions of Agrippa[24] that officials could build without much involvement by the emperor. We cannot, however, support this argument since we know that there was a hiatus in building during the reign of Tiberius. So parsimonious was Tiberius that no public building was possible without his patronage. A bureaucracy could not have developed much strength during a reign when financial control prevented the exercise of power.

Furthermore, we note as evidence of the bias in the original sources against Caligula that the writers seem to blame his prodigious expenditure-rate on riotous living. Maybe so, but it takes a lot of "new sorts of baths" even in "perfumed oil" (Suet. *Calig.* 37) to equal a mile or so of aqueduct! We suspect that the non-visible aqueducts—they would at the start be far out of town where the ancient writers could not see them—were the most important money-users, by far.

CLAUDIUS

Pigors suggests that a dictator is apt to form a new aristocracy who has no claim to power except the dictator's favor rather than to use the more independent members of the old aristocracy who "may be mollified, but who are always dangerous."[25] Claudius epitomizes the dictum. Narcissus, who seems to have had overall directorship of the draining of the Fucine Lake, and Pallas, who seems to have been Claudius' financial man in charge of funding the impressive building programs, were both freedmen, as was the third of Claudius' team of able factotums, Callistus. During the Republic Rome was fortunate as a result of her wars in having a significant number of its slaves and ex-slaves who were trained, educated, and competent; most of these came from the cultured Eastern Mediterranean countries.[26] Under the Empire, however, Rome did not wage war on as large a scale as she had in the preceding centuries. Therefore, she did not get as many captives. Duff discusses the subject:

> So, despite the comparative rarity of Eastern wars, Greek-named slaves predominate to a surprising extent. If war was not their source, whence did they come? The only reasonable hypothesis is that they were descended from the slaves of the Republican age, and that among that class the birth-rate was higher than is generally supposed.[27]

Columella (*RR* 1.8.19), an authority on the first century of the Empire, says that slaves in the *familia rustica* were not only allowed to have children but were encouraged to do so. Tenney Frank examined in Rome five hundred names of imperial freedman on inscriptions where he found 353 Greek ones and 147 Latin ones. Thus, epigraphy suggests that, directly or indirectly, the Orient continued to be the main source of slaves.[28] Duff stresses that the slaves of Greek descent whether from Greece, Asia Minor, Syria or Egypt were unusually intelligent and cultured.[29] It was from such sources that Rome could draw competent people.

Thus, the institution of slavery provided competent people unconstrained by Roman tradition from whom the emperor could select the best talent. As a result, Claudius could successfully find talent and competence in a class of people who had nothing to gain except through absolute loyalty to the emperor for whom they worked and who had absolutely no chance of dynastic succession. As might be expected, the senators and equites resented the transfer of power to social nonentities. As a result, the sources, socially prominent themselves, give the emperor an undeserved reputation for incompetence. Pliny, for example, says (*Pan.* 88.2): "The chief sign of an insignificant emperor is great freedmen." Fergus Millar seems to agree;[30] most modern management theorists would disagree. To them, the sign of greatness is successful delegation. In Claudius' case we have already taken our position: Claudius was at least the second best of the Julio-Claudians, and if he was made so by his freedmen, it is no disgrace. Our position, of course, rests solely on our analysis of public building, but the kind of building Claudius accomplished was almost certainly the highest priority the emperor had at the time. To succeed at his water and food projects was to be a great emperor. The secret of the success of the freedman system is that, first, the emperor must have no delusions about his own omnipotence and, second, enough competence to hunt out men to do the job under *his* guidance. He makes final decisions, but he listens before he decides. We have an excellent example of decision-making by Claudius' team from Tacitus (*Ann.* 11.23–24). Another excellent example of Claudius' doing his own thinking is found in Tacitus (*Ann.* 12.1):

> The emperor, who inclined now one way, now another, as he listened to this, or that advisor, summoned the disputants to a conference and bade them express their opinions and give their reasons.

As Oost notes:

> Significantly in this case he follows the suggestion of Pallas and rejects that of Narcissus, despite the fact that all the evidence for the previous years of his reign points to the latter's occupying the position of highest trust and honor, and despite the fact that Narcissus has just preserved his life and throne. Claudius did have a mind of his own.[31]

The usefulness of the system of using freedmen for key positions in the imperial family seems to have been a short-lived phenomenon. The key task of factotum, starting with the Flavians, returned to the equites order, for reasons which are not certain.[32] Some conjecture is possible. For example, the careers of the freedmen had been so visible, and their rewards so obvious, that higher social classes became willing to subjugate their personal politics to loyalty to the emperor where the rewards were greater. In another vein, freedmen factotums were vigorously opposed by the higher social orders, for obvious reasons: perhaps the united opposition of senators and equites was able to dissuade emperors from reaching so low. But there is another possibility. As we stated earlier a successful freedman system requires a large pool of trained, alert and competent freedmen from which the emperor could choose. The process of selecting out for manumission had been proceeding at a rapid pace since the Empire began and before. As Treggiari says of the last century of the Republic: "We see a new prominence of the *ordo libertinus* in political life and the rise of the individual freedmen . . . which seem to indicate a high degree of political awareness in the freedman, and a high level of competence, drive, and even patriotism."[33] By the end of the Julio-Claudian period this "selection in" process may have run its course and the offspring of the *libertini* have carried the tradition of competence into the main stream of free-born citizens, leaving behind the less talented failures who no longer were as good a source for successful future freedmen.

In conclusion, we believe that Claudius managed his building programs well because he selected his freedmen carefully and effectively.

NERO

Unlike any of the other Julio-Claudians, Nero inherited both a set of factotums and an incubus to help him on his way. Since he was but 16 years old at the time of his accession, he was assigned Burrus and Seneca as his guardians and factotums. The incubus was his mother, who had delusions of being Rome's first "petticoat emperor." (See Tac. *Ann.* [13.5] and *BMC Emp*. I Pl. 38, 1–3) Agrippina, the incubus, early made an effort to do the ruling but was quickly outmaneuvered by Nero's official watchdogs. Burrus was Commander of the Praetorian Guard, thus theoretically a dangerous man to be given too much power. Both Burrus and Seneca had been born equestrians, but Seneca had already achieved the Senate.

It took Nero five years to get rid of his mother; Nero's men had staged a shipwreck first, but Agrippina was too good a swimmer, and they had to use a sword.

As to Seneca and Burrus, they have been lauded as having given Nero a split reign—a quinquennium of good government and then, after they were gone, a poor job. From the viewpoint of his building programs, the facts are, if anything, reversed. It is true that Nero probably had all he could handle with his manpower pool until A.D. 62 when the harbor of Ostia was finished. Aside from that he did nothing of interest in his first five years— not an impressive building record. In A.D. 62, immediately after finishing the Harbor project, however, he started out on his major Thermae project, almost certainly the highest remaining project on the "eat, drink and be merry" agenda. But at the same time he also lost his leading factotum Burrus by death; Seneca, the remaining one, having lost power, seemed to withdraw from the political scene (Tac. *Ann.* 14.52–57). Thus, if Nero had an outstanding quinquennium, it was not the first five years, and it was not due to the work of his two factotums.

Why did Nero get so little payoff from his factotums? In general, factotums have so far in our analysis been extremely valuable to their chiefs, at least for an appreciable time; factotums do not get into trouble until they get ideas of enlarging their role and forget to whom they owe loyalty.

The most obvious answer is that Nero had not personally picked Seneca and Burrus; they were appointed for him. Since a key requirement for a successful factotum is sensitivity to his master's needs, it is not at all surprising that they did Nero little good. Seneca was a Stoic; Nero was not!

As to Burrus, he was, again, a Praetorian Commander, thus a source of Imperial concern. Nero got rid of him probably by poison (Tac. *Ann.* 14.51.1). His place as Praetorian Prefect was taken by Tigellinus, who seemed then to have been involved in getting rid of Nero (Tac. *Hist.* 1.72.1-2).

An interesting parallel with Tiberius; both of them murdered their Praetorian Commanders whose successors then murdered them!

When we consider that Nero had to contend with the great fire in A.D. 64, his performance in building was fully adequate. One would suspect he had a factotum to do his renovation and building (e.g., the Domus Aurea) but we were unable to find one who fits the definition.

CONCLUSIONS

One of the objectives of this book is to find out whether leaders performed, as Syme suggests, from the inevitability of events or whether the rulers created their own world through their personal decisions. From our observations in their building programs, we believe that the rulers are sometimes the driving force. Augustus created the system that allowed him to accomplish his goals; his system, created by his own political genius, was so successful that it prevented Rome from fragmenting, as previous empires had, into oblivion. On the other hand, Tiberius, a man of no vision or political innovativeness, held back the world by his own inertia for nearly twenty-five years, *solus et senex*. As for other Julio-Claudians, we cannot be so confident. Claudius had an established program to follow; had he not done what was done, someone else would have. Caligula was an interlude, and Nero was strictly transitional. Our conclusion to the basic question: Is the personality of the ruler the driving force?

Although the evidence is rather ambiguous, on balance, we believe that the personality of the individual emperors had a strong impact on the building policy of their reigns. If we look at the policy of each emperor, we can see that the ruler's part in the management of building programs changes with each ruler's imperatives. Augustus illustrates this point best. As a man charged with a total rewrite of the *mos maiorum,* he had to concentrate his personal attention on those things which were highly and immediately visible. He had to have his name in the public's mind; thus, his personal attention went to quickly noticeable temples, altars and arches, to statues, porticoes, and monuments: these were flamboyant, inexpensive in manpower and quickly built. Augustus did not neglect the fundamental needs, but for these politically less visible projects (aqueducts) he delegated responsibility to his factotums; so much so that, when his factotums were inactive, he seems to have lost direction. With the death of Agrippa, Augustus' building program collapsed. His power had been consolidated so that he no longer needed the public visibility and his new factotum Tiberius was a nonperformer.

In the case of Tiberius, evidence of an emperor's powerful control of building programs is almost unassailable. He actively and intentionally decided not to build. In spite of obvious problems, particularly in the food supply, he saved his money.

In the case of Caligula, we are less certain. His reign was short and its written evidence is not helpful, but, since a sudden massive increase in building was coincident with Caligula's accession to power, this drastic change is strongly suggestive of his influence.

In the case of Claudius, we believe that he was unquestionably in full control, although he was aided by some capable freedman factotums. Obviously the freedmen would have been helpless to set policy without Claudius' attentive and continuous direction.

In the case of Nero, he inherited from Claudius a major project (the Harbor of Ostia) which he completed. However, once he had completed the projects of Claudius, he unhesitatingly embarked on a building policy of his own.

In conclusion, we would say that the personality of the ruler was the underlying factor in the Julio-Claudian building programs.

ENDNOTES TO CHAPTER VIII

[1]*The General Theory of Employment Interest and Money* (New York, 1936), 121.

[2]Keynes, 126.

[3]Keynes, 131.

[4]Strong, 98.

[5]Strong, 100.

[6]Strong, 100.

[7]According to Webster, a kitchen cabinet is "an unofficial and informal group of advisors to the head of a government who are held to have more influence than his official cabinet."

[8]R. P. Saller, *Personal Patronage Under the Early Empire* (Cambridge, 1982), 8–11; 15; 22; 29.

[9]*Leadership or Domination* (U.S.A., 1935), 116–117.

[10]Meyer Reinhold, *Marcus Agrippa* (Geneva, N.Y., 1933), 20; 22.

[11]Syme, *RR*, 343 states: "Agrippa had been through all the wars of the Revolution—and had won most of them. With exemplary modesty the victor of Naulochus and Actium declined honors and triumphs . . ."

[12]Shipley, *Building Activites*, 19–34.

[13]Reinhold, 12; Jean-Michel Roddaz, *Marcus Agrippa* (Paris, 1984), 32.

[14]Reinhold, 98, considers Agrippa at this time to be co-regent.

[15]Reinhold, 78, suggests that "Augustus did not have sufficient confidence in the judgment of an inexperienced youth [Marcellus], whose competence to control the machinery of the vast empire was as yet untested."

[16]Reinhold, 6. In addition, T. Robert S. Broughton, *The Magistrates of the Roman Republic* (New York, 1951), Vol. 1, xii, states: "In the later period there are reliable records not of the major magistrates only but of the minor officials as well. The lists of magistrates, promagistrates and commands reported in Livy from 218 to 167 B.C. appear to be almost entirely trustworthy."

[17]Broughton, Vol. 2, 636.

[18]For more details, see T. P. Wiseman, *New Men in the Roman Senate 139 B.C.–A.D. 14* (London, 1971), 168–173.

[19]Wiseman, 173.

[20]Levick, 83.

[21]*Virgile et les Origines d'Ostie* (Paris, 1917) 738.

[22]Translated by A. J. Church and W. J. Brobribb, *Complete Works of Tacitus* (New York, 1942), 168.

[23]Translated by Earnest Cary, Loeb Classical Library VI (1968), 357; 359.

[24]Strong, 104.

[25]Pigors, 117.

[26]Susan Treggiari, *Roman Freedmen*, 2–3; S. Oost, "The Career

of Antonius Pallas,'' *AJP* 79 (1958), 115.

[27]A. M. Duff, *Freedmen in the Early Roman Empire* (Oxford, 1928), 3.

[28]Tenney Frank, "Race Mixture in the Roman Empire," *AHR* 21 (1917), 689ff.

[29]Duff, 9.

[30]*The Emperor in the Roman World* (31 B.C.–A.D. 337) (London, 1977), 81.

[31]Oost, 123.

[32]P.R.C. Weaver, *Familia Caesaris* (Cambridge, 1972), 281.

[33]Treggiari, 162.

SELECTED BIBLIOGRAPHY

The bibliography is primarily a list of works cited in the notes and appendices. A supplementary list containing further titles appears under Abbreviations. References to encyclopedias and other standard works do not appear here.

Ancient Sources

Translations for ancient writers can readily be found in *Loeb Classical Library.*

Appian	Historian
	Bella Civilia (BC)
Aristotle	Philosopher
	Politica (Ath. Pol.)
Aug.	Augustus, emperor
	Res Gestae Divi Augusti (RG)
Caes.	G. Julius Caesar, historian
	Bellum Gallicum (BG)
Cato	M. Porcius Cato, orator and historian
	De Re Rustica (RR)
Cic.	M. Tullius Cicero, orator and philosopher
	Epistulae ad Atticum (Ad Att.)
	Oratio de Imperio Cn. Pompeii,
	or *Pro Lege Manilia (De Imp. Pomp.)*
	Tusculanae Disputationes (Tusc.)
Col.	Columella, writer on husbandry
	De Re Rustica (RR)
Dio	Dio Cassius, historian
	Roman History
Front.	Sex. Julius Frontinus, engineer
	De Aquaeductibus Urbis Romae (Aq.)
Josephus	Historian
	Antiquitates Judaicae (AJ)
	Bellum Judaicum (BJ)
Juvenal	D. Junius Juvenalis, poet
	Saturae (Sat.)
Livy	Titus Livius, historian
	Ab Urbe Condita
	periochae (Per.), summaries of
	his lost books
Pliny	C. Plinius Secundus (major)
	Historia Naturalis (NH)
Plutarch	Biographer
	Caesar (Caes.)
	Pompeius (Pomp.)

Quint.	M.T. Quintilianus, rhetorician
	Institutiones Oratoriae (Instit.)
Sen.	L. Annaeus Seneca, philosopher and tragedian
	De Beneficiis (Ben.)
	De Brevitate Vitae (De Brev. Vit.)
	De Ira
	Epistulae (Ep.)
Strabo	Geographer
	Geography
Suet.	C. Suetonius Tranquillus, biographer
	Augustus (Aug.)
	Caesar (Caes.)
	Caligula (Calig.)
	Claudius (Claud.)
	Nero
	Tiberius (Tib.)
	Vitellius (Vit.)
Tac.	C. Cornelius Tacitus, historian
	Annales (Ann.)
	Historia (Hist.)
Tert.	Q. Septimius Florens Tertullianus, Church writer
	Apologeticum (Apol.)
Val. Max.	Valerius Maximus, historian
Varro	M. Terentius Varro, writer on husbandry and language
	De Lingua Latina (LL)
	De Re Rustica (RR)
Vell.	P. Velleius Paterculus, historian
	Historiae Romanae

Secondary Sources

Ardaillon, E., *Les mines du Laurion* (Paris, 1897).

Agostinoni, *Il Fucino* (Bergamo, 1908).

Ashby, T., *The Aqueducts of Ancient Rome* (Oxford, 1935).

van Berchem, D. *Les distributions de blé et d'argent à la plebe romaine sous l'empire* (New York, 1975).

Blackmann, D.J., "Ancient Harbours in the Mediterranean," *IJNA* 11.2 (1982), 79–104 and 11.3 (1982), 185–211.

Blake, M.E., *Roman Constructions in Italy from Tiberius through the Flavians* (Washington, D.C., 1959).

Bloch, M., *Slavery and Serfdom in the Middle Ages* (Berkeley, 1975).

Boren, H.C., "The Urban Side of the Gracchan Economic Crisis," *American Historical Review* 63 (1958), 890–902.

Bourne, F., *Public Works of the Julio-Claudians and the Flavians* (Princeton, N.J., 1941).

Braudel, F., *The Mediterranean*, 2 vols. (New York, 1949).

Brisse, A., *The Draining of Lake Fucino*, trans. by V. de Tivoli (Rome, 1876).

Bromehead, C.N., "Mining and Quarrying to the Seventeenth Century," *A History of Technology* II (Oxford, 1956), 2–10.

Broughton, T.R., *The Magistrates of the Roman Republic* (New York, 1951), 2 vols.

Brunt, P.A., "The Army and the Land in the Roman Revolution," *JRS* 52 (1962), 84.

———, "The 'Fiscus' and its Development," *JRS* 61 (1966), 75–91.

———, *Italian Manpower* (Oxford, 1971).

———, "Free Labour and Public Works at Rome," *JRS* 70 (1980), 81–100.

Campbell, J.B., *The Emperor and the Roman Army* (Oxford, 1984).

Carcopino, J., *Virgile et les origines d' Ostie* (Paris, 1917).

Casson, L., *Ships and Seamanship in the Ancient World* (Princeton, 1971).

Cozzo, G., *Ingegneria romana* (Rome, 1928).

Crawford, M.H., "Money and Exchange in the Roman World," *JRS* 40 (1970), 40–48.

Crook, John, *Consilium Principis* (New York, 1975).

Davis, O., *Roman Mines in Europe* (Oxford, 1935).

Duff, A.M., *Freedmen in the Early Roman Empire* (Oxford, 1928).

Duncan-Jones, R., *The Economy of the Roman Empire* (Cambridge, 1974).

Evans, H.B., "Agrippa's Water Plan," *AJA* 86 (1982), 401–416.

Finley, M.I. (ed.), *Slavery in Classical Antiquity* (Cambridge, 1959).

Frank, T., "Race Mixture in the Roman Empire," *AHR* 21 (1917), 689 ff.

———, "The Financial Crisis of 33 A.D." AJP 56 (1935), 336–341.

Garnsey, P. and Saller, R., *The Roman Empire* (Berkeley and Los Angeles, 1987).

Garzetti, A., *From Tiberius to the Antonines* (London, 1974).

Goodchild, R.G., "Harbours, Docks and Lighthouses," in C.J. Singer & others (eds.), *A History of Technology* II (Oxford, 1956), 516–524.

Griffin, M., *Nero: The End of a Dynasty* (New Haven and London, 1984).

Gruen, E., *The Last Generation of the Roman Republic* (Berkeley, Los Angeles, London, 1974).

Healy, J., *Mining and Metallurgy in the Greek and Roman World* (Ithaca, N.Y., 1978).

Hermansen, G., "Domus and Insula in the City of Rome," *Classica et Mediaevalia* (Copenhagen, 1973), 333–337.

Hind, J.G.F., "The Middle Years of Nero's Reign," *Historia* 20 (1971), 488–505.

———, "Is Nero's Quinquennium an Enigma?" *Historia* 24 (1975), 629–630.

Hopkins, K., *Conquerors and Slaves* (Cambridge, 1968).

Hopper, R.J., "The Laurion Mines: A Reconstruction," *Annual of the British School at Athens* 63 (1968), 293–326.

Jones, A.H.M., "The *Aerarium* and the *Fiscus*," *JRS* 40 (1950), 22–29.

Kambanis, M., "Le dessechement du lac Copais par les anciens," *Bulletin de Correspondence Hellénique* (1893), 333 ff.

Keynes, J.M., *The General Theory of Employment Interest and Money* (New York, 1935).

Klemm, F. A., *History of Western Technology* (New York, 1959).

Lanciani, R., *The Ruins and Excavations of Ancient Rome* (New York, 1897- reissued).

Lauffer, S., *Die Bergwerkssklaven von Laurion* (Wiesbaden, 1979).

Lehmann-Hartleben, K., *Die antiken Hafenanlagen des Mittelmeeres* in *Klio,* Beiheft 14 (1923).

Levick, B.M., *Tiberius the Politician* (London, 1976).

Lintott, A.W., *Violence in Republican Rome* (Oxford, 1968).

Liversidge, J., *Everyday Life in the Roman Empire* (London and New York, 1976).

MacKendrick, P., *The Mute Stones Speak* (New York, 1960).

Mattingly, H., *Roman Coins* (London, 1962).

Meiggs, Russell, *Roman Ostia* (Oxford, 1973).

Middleton, J.H., *The Remains of Ancient Rome* (London and Edinburgh, 1892), 2 vols.

Michels, A.K., *Calendar of the Roman Republic* (U.S.A., 1967).

Millar, F., "The Fiscus in the First Two Centuries," *JRS* 53 (1963), 29–42.

———, *The Emperor and the Roman World* (London, 1977).

Momigliano, A., *Claudius: the Emperor and his Achievements* (Cambridge, 1961).

Nash, E., *Pictorial Dictionary of Ancient Rome* (New York, 1968, 2nd edition), 2 vols.

Newbold, R.F., "Some Social and Economic Consequences of the A.D. 64 Fire at Rome," *Latomus* 33 (1974), 858–869.

———, "Social Tensions at Rome in the Early Years of Tiberius' Reign," *Athenaeum* 52 (1974), 110–143.

Oleson, J.P., *Bronze Age Greek and Roman Technology* (New York and London, 1986).

Oleson, J.P., Hohlfelder, R. and others, "The Caesarea Ancient Harbor Excavation Project," *JFA* 11 (1984), 281–305.

Oost, S., "The Career of Antonius Pallas," *AJP* 79 (1958), 113–139.

Packer, J.E., "Housing and Population in Imperial Ostia and Rome," *JRS* (1967), 80–95.

Paget, R.F., "The Ancient Ports of Cumae," *JRS* 58 (1968), 152–169.

Pigors, P., *Leadership or Domination* (U.S.A., 1935).

Platner, S.B. and Ashby, T., *A Topographical Dictionary of Ancient Rome* (London, 1929).

Reinhold, M., *Marcus Agrippa* (Geneva, New York, 1933).

Roddaz, J., *Marcus Agrippa* (Paris, 1984).

Rickman, G., *The Corn Supply of Ancient Rome* (Oxford, 1971).

Rodewald, C., *Money in the Age of Tiberius* (Manchester, 1976).

Saller, R.P., *Personal Patronage Under the Early Empire* (Cambridge, 1982).

Savile, L., "Ancient Harbours," *Antiquity* 15 (1941), 208–132.

Schumpeter, J., *Business Cycles* (New York, 1939).

Shipley, F.W., *Agrippa's Building Activities In Rome* (St. Louis, 1933).

Sippel, Donald V., "Some Observations on the Means and Cost of the Transport of Bulk Commodities in the Late Republic and Early Empire," *The Ancient World* 16 (1987), 35–45.

————, "Dietary Deficiency Among the Lower Classes of Late Republican and Early Imperial Rome," *The Ancient World* 16 (1987), 47–54.

Smallwood, E.M., *Documents Illustrating the Principates of Gaius, Claudius, and Nero* (Cambridge, 1967).

Strong, D.E., "The Administration of Public Building in Rome During the Late Republic and Early Empire," *Institute of Classical Studies Bulletin* 15 (1968), 97–109.

Sutherland, C.H.V., *Coinage in Roman Imperial Policy 31* B.C.–A.D. *68* (New York, 1951, reprinted 1971).

————, *The Emperor and the Coinage: Julio-Claudian Studies* (London, 1976).

Sydenham, E.A., *The Coinage of Nero* (London, 1920).

Syme, R., *The Roman Revolution* (Oxford, 1939).

Testaguzza, O., "The Port of Rome," *Archaeology* 17 (1964), 173–179.

————, *Portus* (Rome, 1970).

Thornton, M.K., "Nero's New Deal," *TAPA* 102 (1971), 621–629.

————, "The Enigma of Nero's *Quinquennium*," *Historia* 22 (1973) 570–582.

————, "Augustan Tradition and Neronian Economics," *ANRW* II (1975), 149–175.

————, "Julio-Claudian Building Programs: Eat, Drink, and Be Merry," *Historia* 35 (1986), 28–44.

Thornton, M.K. and Thornton, R.L., "Manpower Needs for the Public Works Programs of the Julio-Claudian Emperors," *Journal of Economic History* XLIII, No. 2 (June, 1983), 373–378.

————, "The Draining of the Fucine Lake: A Quantitative Analysis," *The Ancient World* 12 (1985), 105–120.

Treggiari, S., *Roman Freedmen During the Late Republic* (Oxford, 1969).

Van Deman, E.B., *The Building of the Roman Aqueducts* (Washington, D.C., 1934).

Vogt, J., *Ancient Slavery and the Ideal of Man* (Cambridge, Mass., 1975).

Weaver, P.R.C., *Familia Caesaris* (Cambridge, 1972).

Westerman, W.L., *The Slave Systems of Greek and Roman Antiquity* (Philadelphia, 1955).

White, K.D., *Greek and Roman Technology* (Ithaca, New York, 1984).

Wiedemann, T., *Greek and Roman Slavery* (Baltimore and London, 1981).

William, P.F., "Roman Harbours," *IJNA* 5 (1976), 73–79.

Wilson, F.H., "Studies in Social and Economic History of Ostia," *BSR* 13 (1935) 14; 14 (1938) 152.

Wiseman, T.P., *New Men in the Roman Senate 139* B.C.–A.D. *14* (London, 1971).

Yavetz, Z., *Plebs and Princeps* (Oxford, 1969).

APPENDIX 1

Method of Determining the WUs for Certain Other Constructions:

PORTICOES

We used a portico to evaluate WUs assigned to certain major projects. First we need to explain how we did this: We evaluated the porticoes as follows: We considered that the building of a portico (columns and a roof only) had much less work involved in its construction than a temple. Thus, we concluded that 100 meters of portico was ⅓ of the standard temple or $\frac{60}{3}$ = 20 WUs. When sizes of all porticoes of the period on which we had data are averaged, the average length is 323 meters; an insufficiently described portico is evaluated as an average portico of 323 meters and given 65 WUs.

MAJOR CONSTRUCTIONS

A different approach was used for three types of construction of major importance: the imperial domus, the theatre, and the aqueduct. Each one required special consideration.

Domus

For the Domus Aurea we used the measurements of its basic palace area at the basic temple rate:

$$\frac{215 \times 55}{8 \text{ (temple rate)}} = \frac{11825}{8} = 1478 \text{ WUs}$$

Plus, its colonnade
1 mile at 20 WUs = $\frac{10.00}{.6 \text{ (Eng. mile)}}$ × 20WUs (Portico rate) = 333WUs

Basic Palace + 1478WUs
1811WUs

Within the park decorations (a guess)   189WUs
2000WUs

Theaters

For the theater, we used the measurement for the Theater of Marcellus as our basic unit. Other theaters were compared to the Theater of Marcellus in accordance with their seating capacity. We used two ways of calculating work units for the Theater of Marcellus. First, we thought that we might count the arches; there were three stories of 40 arches each at our standard of 25 WUs per arch. Its WU value, based on these calculations, would be 3000. As an alternate approach, we used the measurement of its diameter – 150 meters:

Calculations

Diameter − 150 m; ∴ radius (r) = 75 m

π = 3.14

Area of semicircle (shape of theater) = ½ of area of circle

Formula:

$$\frac{\text{Area of}}{\text{theater}} = \frac{\pi \times r \times r}{2} = \frac{3.14 \times 75 \text{ m} \times 75 \text{ m}}{2} = 8,831 \text{ m}^2$$

1 WU = 8 m^2

Formula:

$$\text{Work units} = \frac{\text{area of theater}}{8 \text{ m}^2} = \frac{8,831 \text{ m}^2}{8 \text{ m}^2} = 1,104 \text{ WUs}$$

There are two stories (average − 3 on the perimeter; 1 on the inside)

1,104 WUs × 2 = 2,208 WUs

We used the 2nd method in our calculations.

Aqueducts

For aqueducts, first, we set the work involved in making an extremely expensive private house by comparison with the imperial domus. The Domus Transitoria was 1,000 WUs; the Domus Aureus, 2,000; the House of Augustus (literary sources say unpretentious), 98; The Domus Tiberiana, 1,350. The house in question was that of Clodius on the Palatine and was described as "worthy of the madness of Kings" (Pliny, *NH* 36.5). We set it at 500 WUs, and knew its construction cost from Pliny to be 15 million sesterces. We also knew from Pliny (*NH* 36.122) that the Anio Novus and the Aqua Claudia cost 350 million sesterces.

By proportion: (if 15 million sesterces buy 500 WUs worth, how much will 350 million sesterces buy?)

Trial I   15:500 : : 350: X
           X = 11,666WUs for combined Anio Novus
           and Claudia

The combined length of the 2 aqueducts is 156 kilometers;

So:

$$\frac{11,666}{156} = 75 \text{ WUs per Kilometer}$$

Trial II   Using the *Marcia*, constructed in 144–140 BC as a base, we knew that it cost 180 million sesterces (Front. *Aq.* 1.7).

Then, if 15 million sesterces produces 500 WUs [see Trial I], 180 million sesterces should produce 6000 WUs.

15 : 500 : : 180: X
X = 6000

The Marcia is 91 km long;

$$\frac{6000}{91} = 66 \text{WUs per Kilometer}$$

Considering the date difference and the more advanced construction of the later aqueducts, the figures are quite compatible. We then did an *outside* comparison for compatibility.

Problem: 1 km. of portico   = 200WUs

but

1 km. of Aqueduct = 70WUs (+ or −)

We believed the 70 WU figure was too low, subjectively, considering the construction differences between porticoes and aqueducts. We then reviewed our *comparison base* (the domus at 15 million sesterces) and believed the domus price to be inflated by *location* (it was on the Palatine), independent of manpower cost, causing the proportion to work out *lower* than was appropriate. We estimated, for final use, aqueduct labor cost at 100 WUs per kilometer, one half of the portico cost for the same distance.

Having established the basic WUs for the aqueduct, we assigned work units to each one; Frontinus's treatise, *de aquis* (with refinements), gives us accurate measurements for each aqueduct as the following chart shows:

Name	Distance in meters	Work units to build
Aqua Appia[1]	16,444	1644
Anio Vetus[1]	63,704	6370
Marcia[1]	91,424	9142
Tepula[1]	17,745	1774
Julia[1]	22,853	2285
Virgo[2]	22,954	2295
Alsietina[1]	32,814	3281
Claudia[3]	68,680	6868
(1) Arcus Neronianus[4]	2000	400
Anio Novus[5]	86,876	8687

[1]Lanciani, 58.
[2]Van Deman, 169.
[3]Front. *Aq.* 1.14.
[4]Van Deman, 14. Because it was inside the city and carried on high arches, we doubled its WU cost.
[5]Front. *Aq.* 1.15.

APPENDIX 2

List of All Julio-Claudian Building Projects Examined, Evaluated, and Quantified

Date	Description	Work	Work Units
Augustus	Extends Pomerium	Minor	0
Augustus	Reclaims Campus Esquilinus	Reclaims	1
Augustus	Rostra	Enlarges	5
Augustus	Temple of Diana	Builds	60
A.D. 12	Temple of Flora	Restores	13
29–28 B.C.	Temple of Juno Regina	Restores	40
29–28 B.C.	Temple of the Lares	Restores	40
29–28 B.C.	Temple of Minerva on the Aventine	Restores	50
29–28 B.C.	Temple of the Penates	Restores	40
Augustus	Clivus Palatinus	Paves	79
Augustus	Clivus Capitolinus	Paves	23
Augustus	Arch of Octavian	Erects	25
29 B.C.	Pulvinar in Circus Maximus	Builds	3
Augustus	Porticus ad Nationes	Builds	65
Augustus	Statues from Capitol to Campus Martius	Removes	0
Augustus	Auditorium of Maecenas	Builds	32
Augustus	Statue of Apollo in Vicus Sandalarius	Erects	0
29 B.C.	Temple of Divus Julius	Dedicates	10
29 B.C.	Curia Julia	Dedicates	6
29 B.C.	Statue and Altar of Victory	Erects	8
29 B.C.	Atrium Libertatis	Restores	6
29 B.C.	Chalcidicum	Builds	15
29 B.C.	Temple of Hercules Musarum	Restores	60
29 B.C.	Porticus Philippi	Builds	46
29 B.C.	Arch of Augustus	Erects	25
29 B.C.	Amphitheater of Statius Taurus	Builds	120
29 B.C.	House of M. Antonius on Palatine	Burnt	0
29 B.C.	Buys and Rebuilds House of Catulus	Rebuilds	30
Augustus	Temple of Apollo Palatinus	Dedicates	7
29–27 B.C.	Mausoleum of Augustus	Builds	120
28 B.C.	Temporary Wooden Stadium of Augustus	Builds	10
27–25 B.C.	Pantheon of Agrippa	Builds	108
29–27 B.C.	House of Augusta	Rebuilds	98
27 B.C.	Porticus of Octaviae	Builds	98

Date	Description	Work	Work Units
28–26 B.C.	Temple of Jupiter Captolinus	Restores	174
29–26 B.C.	Saepta	Completes and Dedicates	594
26–25 B.C.	Porticus Argonautarum	Builds	60
25–19 B.C.	Thermae	Builds	1125
26–25 B.C.	Basilica Neptuni	Builds	107
25 B.C.	Horrea Agrippiana	Builds	40
26–25 B.C.	Temple of Bonus Eventus	Builds	100
25 B.C	Stagnum Agrippae	Builds	30
26–25 B.C.	Bridge by Agrippa	Builds	125
25 B.C.	Porticus Vipsania	Builds	40
23 B.C.	Library in Porticus Octavia	Established	10
Augustus	Forum	Paves	32
23–22 B.C.	Temple of Jupiter Tonans	Builds	100
21 B.C.	Pons Fabricius	Restores	28
42–2 B.C.	Temple of Mars Ultor	Builds	184
20 B.C.	Miliarium Aureum	Erects	2
24–19 B.C.	Aqua Virgo	Completes	2295
19 B.C.	Altar of Fortuna Redux	Builds	5
19 B.C.	Second Arch of Augustus in Forum	Erects	30
18–13 B.C.	Theater of Marcellus	Builds	2208
16 B.C.	Temple of Juventas	Restores	40
16 B.C.	Porticus around Temple of Quirinus	Builds	66
15 B.C.	Crypta Balbi	Builds	275
15–7 B.C.	Porticus Liviae	Builds and Dedicates	76
14 B.C.	Temples of Jupiter Stator and Juno Regina	Restores	60
15–14 B.C.	Basilica Aemilia	Rebuilds	182
13–12 B.C.	Theater of Balbus	Builds	1790
13 B.C.	Ara Pacis	Builds	30
12–11 B.C.	Pons Aemilius	Restores	97
11 B.C.	Fornix Augusti	Restores	25
11 B.C.	Domus Publica	Gives	0
11 B.C.	Horti of Agrippa	Builds	10
11 B.C.	Shrine of Vesta of Palatine	Builds	10
11 B.C.	Tomb of C. Cestius	Builds	30
11–4 B.C.	Restores Aqueducts	Restores	8487
11–4 B.C.	Alsietina Aqueduct	Constructs	3281
10 B.C.	Obelisk in Campus Martius and in Circus	Sets up	10
9 B.C.	Pedestal to Vulcan	Dedicates	2
16–15 B.C.	Temple of Concord	Builds	135
7 B.C.	Temple of Concord	Rebuilds	36
8 B.C.	Arch to Drusus the Elder	Builds	15
10–8 B.C.	Cohortes Vigilium	Builds	360
8 B.C.	Terminal Stones of Tiber	Sets up	5

Date	Description	Work	Work Units
7 B.C.	Divides Rome into 14 Regions	Divides	0
6 B.C.	Temple of Consus	Restores	40
10–7 B.C.	Diribitorium	Builds	394
7 B.C.	Campus Agrippa	Builds	10
7 B.C.	Basilica Opimia	Removes	11
7 B.C.	Macellum Liviae	Builds	80
7 B.C.	Terminal Stones-Tiber	Sets up	5
5 B.C.	Arch over Via Tiburtina	Rebuilds	9
2 B.C.	Water to Circus Flaminus	Arranges	10
2 B.C.	Forum of Augustus	Builds	396
2 B.C.	Naumachia Augusti	Constructs	100
2 B.C.	Basilica Aemilia	Inscribes	0
A.D. 2	Garden of Maecenas	Takes Residence	0
A.D. 2	Arch of Lentulus and Crispus	Builds	15
A.D. 3	Temple of Magna Mater	Restores	28
A.D. 3	Horti Lamiani	Builds	10
A.D. 3	House of Augustus	Rebuilds	98
A.D. 6	Temple of Castor	Rebuilds	113
A.D. 7	Altar of Ceres Mater and Ops Augusta	Builds	5
A.D. 9	Temple of Isis	Destroys	10
A.D. 9	Temple of Bona Dea Subsaxana	Restores	40
A.D. 10	Arch of Dolabella and Silanus	Builds	15
7 B.C. - A.D. 12	Basilica Julia	Rebuilds and Enlarges	495
A.D. 14	Aqua Julia	Restores	913
A.D. 14	Temple of Ceres and Libra	Restores	14
Augustus	Entrance to Lupercal	Repairs	10
Augustus	Altar and Shrine to Mercury	Builds	5
Augustus	Canopy over Forum	Erects	0
Augustus	Temple of Jupiter Libertas on the Aventine	Restores	40
Tiberius	Temple of Augustus	Builds	112
Tiberius	Library	Builds	10
Tiberius	Domus Tiberiana	Builds	1350
Tiberius	Schola Xanthi	Builds	30
A.D. 15	Repair of Cippi	Repair	20
A.D. 16	Arch of Tiberius	Builds	25
A.D. 16	Chapel of Gens Julia	Builds	10
A.D. 15–16	Temple of Fors Fortuna	Erects	100
A.D. 15–17	Temple of Flora	Restores	27
A.D. 17	Temple of Ceres, Liber & Libera	Restores	29
A.D. 17	Temple of Janus	Reconstructs	20
A.D. 17	Temple of Spes	Restores	22
A.D. 19	Arch of Germanicus	Erects	25
A.D. 18–19	Arches of Drusus & Germanicus	Erects	50
A.D. 22–37	Theater of Pompey	Restores	884
A.D. 21–23	Castra Praetoria	Builds	804

Date	Description	Work	Work Unit
A.D. 22–23	Basilica Aemilia	Restores	182
A.D. 22	Ara Pietatis Augustae	Vows	0
A.D. 22	Facade of Carcer	Builds	5
A.D. 24	Arch of Drusus the Younger	Erects	25
A.D. 28	Altar to Amicitia of Tiberius	Dedicates	5
A.D. 28	Altar to Clementia of Tiberius	Erects	5
A.D. 34	Part of Cloaca Maxima	Rebuilds	4
A.D. 36	Part of Circus Maximus	Repairs	20
A.D. 36–37	Cippi of Aqua Virgo	Erects	0
A.D. 39–40	Temple to sister Drusilla	Builds	40
A.D. 38–40	Three temples	Builds	180
Caligula	Amphitheater	Begins	100
A.D. 38–39	Circus Gai et Neronis	Built	30
Caligula	Temple ofAugustus	Dedicates	12
Caligula	Domus Tiberiana	Extends	1350
A.D. 39	Bridge to Capitol	Builds	20
A.D. 37–52	Aqua Claudia	Builds	6868
A.D. 37–52	Anio Novus	Builds	8688
Claudius	Altar-Temple of Jupiter Depulsor	Erects	5
Claudius	Temple of Felicitas burnt	Not rebuilt	0
Claudius	Temple of Salus burnt	Restored Later	0
Claudius	Arch of Tiberius	Builds	25
Claudius	Porticus Minucia Frumentaria	Builds	65
Claudius	Statues in Temple of Augustus	Erects	15
Claudius	Horti Pallantiani	Builds	10
Claudius	Terminal Stones of Tiber	Erects	15
A.D. 43	Ara Pietatis Augustae	Erects	5
Claudius	Cippi of Aqua Virgo	Erects	0
A.D. 51–52	Arch of Claudius	Builds	15
A.D. 46–54	Aqua Virgo	Restores	918
A.D. 52	Porta Praenestina (Maggiore)	Builds	30
Claudius	Colossus of Jove	Erects	50
A.D. 55–61	Domus Transitoria	Builds	1000
Nero	Euripus in Circus Maximus	Removes	50
A.D. 55–60	Temple of Claudius	Half Builds	60
A.D. 60	Arch of Nero	Erects	25
A.D. 58–61	Macellum Magnum	Builds	111
A.D. 62	Trophies of Nero	Displays	5
A.D. 61–62	Gymnasium of Nero	Builds	100
A.D. 62–64	Thermae Neronianae	Builds	2850
A.D. 63	Temple of Fecunditas	Vows	0
A.D. 65–68	Domus Aurea	Builds	2000
A.D. 66–67	Temple of Fortuna Sejani	Builds	100
A.D. 67–68	Colossus of Nero	Erects	100
A.D. 66	Porticus (generally called Margaritaria)	Builds	40
Nero	Temple of Claudius	Destroys	0
A.D. 65	Circus Maximus	Rebuilds	60

Date	Description	Work	Work Units
A.D. 65	Wooden Amphitheater	Builds	72
A.D. 65–67	House of the Vestals	Rebuilds	618
Nero	Campus Neronis	Floods	0
Nero	Arcus Neroniani	Builds	400
A.D. 64	Pavement of Clivus Palatinus	Paves	90
A.D. 65–66	Pons Neronianus	Builds	125
Nero	Balneum Tigellini	Builds (?)	0
Nero	Rivus Herculaneus	Destroys	0
A.D. 68	Heroum to Poppaea	Built	15

APPENDIX 3
Fucine Lake

This appendix provides the basic facts, assumptions, calculations and conclusions behind the statements made in the main body of the study.

Facts

a. The Roman Tunnel was 6180 yards long (Brisse, p. 30). Its cross section was 11.9 yards^2 (Brisse p. 16).

b. The tunnel was built by first digging 40 shafts (Brisse p. 18), down from the surface to an average depth of 196 feet (Brisse, Plate IV measured and averaged by the authors). Workmen then drove the tunnel horizontally along the surveyed path in both directions from the foot of each shaft until they met the corresponding face being driven from the shafts next in line along the route.

c. Air shafts (*cuniculi*) driven from the surface to intersect the main shafts at various depths ventilated the underground works. The *cuniculi* totalled at length "at least double that of the main tunnel" (Brisse, p. 23) taken by the authors to mean 2.25 times the length of the main tunnel.

d. Shafts were 14.16 feet in cross section (Brisse, p. 19).

e. Four men using two capstans removed the spoil up through the shaft (Daremberg, Fig. 2662; Brisse, p. 20).

f. For about 3518 yards the tunnel was excavated through compact rock without revetment; for 2662 yards it was lined with strong masonry (Brisse, 94; 139).

g. Debris was raised from the tunnel to the surface in a bucket with the capacity of 1.4 feet^3 (Brisse, 20). One of these buckets was found at the bottom of a shaft (Brisse, 20).

Assumptions

1. Two men, working on a rock face, either horizontally or vertically, could free 30 feet^3 of rock or other material in one 9 to 10 hour day. Basis: Bromehead (p.3). Forbes (p. 153) would support 30 feet^3 in a mine shaft digging situation.

2. The work was organized as one shift, 9–10 hour day. From our own internal calculations shift working, while making Suetonius' "30,000" men less unlikely, would have made his "11 continuous years" much too long. Of Suetonius' two parameters, the "11 years" is highly probable; the "30,000 men," much less so.

3. The work was performed on a basis of "cut, trim and clean" as laborers went along a tunnel or down a shaft. To rough cut a small passage, then put several men to enlarge the passage would *increase* the number of men needed per work crew, but would create nearly insoluble problems of detritus removal.

4. There were 316 working days per year (Michels, p. 68).

5. Broken rock is carried in baskets .656 feet in diameter by .558 feet in height (Davies, p. 30).

6. The cross section of the *cuniculi* had the same dimensions as a shaft.

Calculations

1. Volume of rock to be processed
A. Tunnel
Data:
Length—6,180 yds.
Cross-section—11.9 yds.^{2}
27 ft^3 per yd.^{3}
6,180 yds. x 11.9 yds.^{2} × 27 ft.^{3} per yd.^{3} =   1,985,634 ft.^{3}

B. Shafts—Main:
Data:
Average length—196 ft.
Number of shafts— 40
Cross section of shaft 14.16 ft. × 14.16 ft.
196 ft. x 14.16 ft. × 14.16 ft. × 40 =   1,571,964 ft.^{3}

Shafts—Accessory and *Cuniculi*
Data:
Tunnel length—6,180 yds.
Ratio of *cuniculi* length to shaft length—2.25
Cross section of *cuniculi*—14.16 × 14.16 ft.

6,180 yds. × $\dfrac{3 \text{ ft.}}{\text{yd.}}$ × 2.25 × 14.16 ft. × 14.16 ft. =

$\overline{\qquad\qquad\qquad\qquad\qquad}$ 8,364,091 ft.^{3}

Total volume to be processed   11,921,689 ft.^{3}

2. Minimum time involved
A. Daily output
Data:
The daily output per face—30 ft.^{3}
Number of shafts— 40 shafts × 2 faces per shaft =   80
                        80 *cuniculi* faces   80
                           Total faces   160

Daily output
160 × 30 ft.^{3} = 4,800 ft.^{3}

B. Days to complete the draining:

$$\frac{\text{Total volume to be processed}}{\text{Gross daily output}} \quad \frac{11,921,689 \text{ ft.}^3}{4,800 \text{ ft.}^3} = 2,848 \text{ days}$$

C. Years to complete the draining:

$$\frac{\text{Total number of days}}{\text{Working days per year}} \quad \frac{2,484 \text{ days}}{316} = 7.86 \text{ years}$$

3. Composition of a shaft-crew (which worked on a shaft plus 2 tunnel segments, one each way from the foot of the shaft).

A. Facers. Each rock face was 11.9 yds.^{2} This would be a square 3.4 yds. on each side, or 10.3 ft. However, the actual cross section was a rectangle with a semi-circular roof with the rectangle in the ratio of 2.10 height to 1.80 width; thus the tunnel should have been about 8 ft. wide, room for no more than two men to work side by side.
2 men per face (2 faces per crew)   **4 men**

B. Basket loaders. Each face team, working two faces, will cut 30 feet^3 of rock per day. Limestone has a specific gravity of 2.5. To calculate a ft.^{3} of limestone:

2.5 x 62.4 (weight of 1 ft.^{3} of water) = 156 lbs.
Daily weight: 156 lbs./ft.^{3} x 30 ft.^{3}/day = 4,680 lbs. per day
Data: The basket used has a radius of .328 ft. and a depth (d) of .558 ft. Volume $\pi r^2 d$

One basket will carry (3.14 x .328^2) x .558 = .188 ft.^{3}
.188 ft.^{3} x 156 lbs. = 29.40 lbs./ft.^{3} per basket (30 rounded)
4,680 total daily lbs. ÷ 30 lbs./basket = 156 baskets per day or about 16 per hour.
1 loader per face (See Bromehead, Fig. 11, p. 2
for a similar task).   **2 men**

C. Porters. Each face porter group (two members) must pick up a 30 lb. basket, carry it an average of 6180 ÷ 40 ÷ 2 (meet in the middle) = 77 yds., deliver the basket to the capstan and return, bearing any inbound material if present. 156 baskets per day; 78 per man or a little over 8 baskets per hour.

2 porters per face team   **4 men**

D. Bucket loader. He takes baskets from porters and dumps in the lift basket. 156 baskets per day.

1 man per face team   **2 men**

E. Capstan men. Each shaft was equipped with 2 capstans (Giuseppe Cozzo, *Ingegneria Romana* [Rome, 1928], Plate IV, Fig. 110). Each capstan has 2 buckets, one going up, one down. Each bucket carries 1.4 cubic ft. or 218 lbs. (Brisse, 20). Each capstan is manned by 2 men (Daremberg and Saglio II/1, p. 602, Fig. 2662). 30 ft.^{3} ÷ 1.4 ft.^{3}/bucket = 21 lifts per day; 2+ per hour.

2 men each of 2 capstans   **4 men**

F. Bucket-Dumpers. We believe the buckets would be gravity dumped into a chute without being removed from the hoist cable. The chute would be movable and arranged to spread the spoil. The land on which it was dumped would be valueless. 2 + buckets per hour.

2 men   **2 men**

G. Utility man. These are provided to cover sick, injured, or small unexpected problems. One of them would probably be the shaft foreman on a working basis when problems occur.

2 men   **2 men**

Summary

Facers	4	men
Basket Loaders	2	
Porters	4	
Bucket Loaders	2	
Capstan Men	4	
Bucket Dumpers	2	
Utility Men	2	
	20 men	

APPENDIX 4
Harbor of Ostia

Organization:

Objective 1 calculates the size of the task: objective 2 calculates the manpower and oxen needs using oxen as sand movers; objective 3 calculates using humans for sand moving.

Objective 1:

To calculate, roughly, the number of cubic feet of sand to move and the organizaton to do so.

1. Otello Testagussa (*Archaeology* 17 (1964), 177) states that the harbor is about 1/3 of a square mile

   1 sq. mile = 5280 x 5280 = 27,878,400 sq. ft.

   1/3 of a sq. mile = $\dfrac{27,878,400}{3}$ = 9,292,800 sq. ft.

2. To get the sides of the square harbor (see 1 above) take the square root of 9,292,800:

   $\sqrt{9,292,800}$ = 3,048 ft. = each side of the harbor.

   We assume that the work will be organized to move sand from the center of the harbor in both directions to the shore where it will be taken an equal distance on land to dump. Thus, the first load will travel half of the width of the harbor within the harbor perimeter and an additional half of the width of the harbor on land. This first load will travel 1,524 ft. + 1,524 ft. On the other hand, the last load (starting at the shore) will travel no distance. Therefore, the loads will move an average of 1,524 ft. The above is charted in **Assumption** (Chart 3).

3. To get the amount of sand needed to be moved, we have presumed a sand profile compared to the finished water level as portrayed in Chart 2, that is, on the landward end of the harbor the sand will be 16.5 ft. above the final sea level; on

145

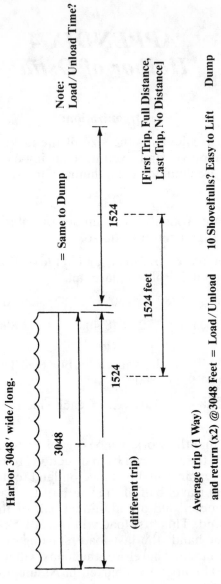

Chart 3. Harbor of Ostia

the seaward end of the harbor the sand will be 16.5 ft. below the sea level.[1] Geometrically, since the two triangles are equal to the amount of sand to move, the amount of sand will equal the width of the square times the length of the square times the finished depth of the harbor. Thus:

$$\text{Sand to be moved} = 3,048 \text{ ft.} \times 3,048 \text{ ft.} \times 16.5 \text{ ft.}$$
$$= 153,331,200 \text{ ft.}^3$$

4. To get the number of trips an ox can travel in one day, we have used the following information: K.D. White says an ox can travel 25 miles per day.[2] On the other hand, Sippel suggests a lower number of miles. Because of Sippel's information we have modified our conclusion from 25 miles per day to 15 miles per day.[3]

$$15 \text{ miles} \times 5,280 \text{ ft. per mile} = 79,200 \text{ ft. per day.}$$

We assume that loading and unloading will take one tenth of the total time so travel feet will be but 79,200 ft. × .9 = 71,280 ft. per day.

Therefore, an ox can make $\dfrac{71,280 \text{ ft.}}{3,048 \text{ ft.}} = \dfrac{23 \text{ trips per day.}}{(2 \text{ above})}$

5. To complete the task, the cubic feet of sand to be moved divided by the cubic feet of sand moved per trip = the no. of ox trips required to dig out the harbor. We assume an ox can carry one cubic foot (156 lbs.) per trip.

$$\frac{153,000,000 \text{ ft.}^3}{23}$$

= 6,652,170 ox-days required to complete the task.

Assuming a 320 work day year, 20,788 ox-years would be required.

$$\frac{6,652,170 \text{ ox days}}{320 \text{ working days}} = 20,788 \text{ ox-years}$$

$$\frac{20,788 \text{ ox years}}{10 \text{ years}} = \frac{2,078 \text{ oxen could do the job}}{\text{in ten years}}$$

It would take about 2,000 oxen to complete the job in 10 years. Sippel has suggested limitation on the use of oxen. If this is so, more ox keepers would be required.[4]

Objective 2: To calculate the manpower and oxen needs using oxen as sand movers.

2000 oxen + supervision (1 supervisor per track)

Ox driver (8 oxen per track)	2000
Supervisor for ox drivers—1 per track	250
Loaders (2) and dumpers (2) 4 per track	1000
General supervision 325	325
Ox keeper (1 man per 8 oxen)	250
Total men to do sand lifting job	3825

Additional men
Mole builders
Quay-makers

Objective 3: To calculate using humans for sand moving.

Manpower needs (human power system)

From objective 1—cu. feet to move	153,331,200
wt. per cu. foot	x 156 lbs.
	23,868,000,000
or	24 billion lbs.

$$\frac{24,000,000,000 \text{ lbs.}}{60 \text{ lbs. per man per trip}^5} = 400,000,000 \text{ Mantrips}$$

A man can make as many trips per day as an ox can: 23

$$\frac{400,000,000}{23} = 17,391,304 \quad \text{Man days}$$

$$\frac{17,391,304}{320} = 54,347 \quad \text{Man year}$$

$$\frac{54,347}{10 \text{ yrs.}} = 5,434 \quad \text{Men could do it in 10 years}$$

Sand moving only → direct labor *only*

ENDNOTES TO APPENDIX 4

[1]We used 16.5 ft. based on information in O. Testagussa, *Portus*, 69, where he stated that the depth was between 4.7 meters and 5.7 meters.

[2]White, *Greek and Roman Tech.*, 131.
[3]Sippel, "Means and Cost of Transport of Bulk Commodities,"
36.
[4]Sippel, 36.
[5]White, *Greek and Roman Tech.*, 128.

INDEX

The numbers in boldface refer to the page numbers of the illustrations.

absolute labor costs, 19, 71.
acta populi, 7.
acta senatus, 7.
Actium, 4.
aediles, role in public building, 32–3, 105, 109.
aerarium, 48.
Africa, 5.
Agrippa xii, 5, 33, 44, 46–7, 109, 116, 121.
  as aedile, 33.
  as factotum, 108–112.
  Vipsanius nomen, 111.
Agrippina, Julia, the Younger, 71, 96, 119.
Aljustrel Tables, 70.
Anderson, J.G.C., 99.
Anio Novus, aqueduct, 23, 25, 51, 59, 72, 113; **30, 52, 94.**
Anio Vetus, aqueduct, 44.
Antony, Mark, 4, 109.
Aqua Alsietina, aqueduct, 6, 25, 43, 46.
Aqua Claudia, aqueduct, 23, 25, 48, 51, 59, 113.
Aqua Julia, aqueduct, 25.
Aqua Marcia, aqueduct, 6, 44.
Aqua Virgo, aqueduct, 6, 25, 41, 43, 46.
aqueduct, see also by individual name, 5–6, 39, 41, 43.
  repair of, 5–6.
  type of labor needs, 44, 72.
  calculation of WUs, 131–4.
  transfer of labor between projects, 72, 95.
Appennines, 59.
Apollonia, 109.
Archaeology, 18.
Ardaillon, E., 64–5.
Ashby, 18.
Augustan Approach, 41–44.
Augustan boom, 25, 41, 46.

Augustan prosperity, 12, 38.
Augustus, Emperor, xii, 3–7, 10–2, 15–8, 21, 32–3, 41–44.
  temple building, 4.
  food supply, 5.
  inflating his building program, 18.
  obtaining control of building, 32–4, 106.
  his building policy, 41–44.
  relationship with factotums, 109–12.
  later building programs and Agrippa's death, 44.
  reorganizing the management structure, 32–3.
  shifting financial supervision, 32, 105.
Aurelius Victor, see Victor

Basilica Aemilia, 19, 32.
Basilica Julia, 25.
Blake, Marion, 22.
Bloch, M., 35.
Bourne, F.C., 4.
Braudel, F., 97.
Brisse, A., 59, 63, 66, 68–9.
Bromehead, C.N., 64–5.
Brunt, P.A., 35–6.
Building projects, detailed evaluations, see Appendix 2, 135–9.
  as an unbiased source, 115–6.
  as a connection with the emperors, x, 120–1.
  list of all Julio-Claudian projects, Appendix 2, 135–9.
Burrus, praetorian prefect, 96, 100, 108, 119–20.
business cycles, 9, 26, 29, 36–9.
  innovation, 38.
  identification, 24–6.

151

Caligula, Emperor, 7, 23, 48, 51,
53, 113–6, 120–1.
  his building policy, 51, 113.
  his relationship with factotums,
  113–6.
  possible historians' bias, 113,
  115.
  possible inflation, 51, 53.
  civil unrest, 53.
  manpower sources, 51.
  role in aqueduct building, 51.
Caligulan Charge, 51, 53.
Callistus (imperial freedman), 96,
  114, 116.
Caesar, Julius, ix, 32–3, 46–7, 53,
  77.
Capri, 112–3.
Carcopino, J., 5, 47, 111.
Carthage, 79.
Cassius Chaerea, 114.
Cassius Dio, see Dio
Castra Praetoria, 25, 113.
Cato, 21.
censors, 31–3.
Cicero, 111.
Circus Maximus, 96.
civil unrest, 5, 53, 96.
Civil War, 6, 41.
Claudian Connections, 53, 93–6;
  92.
Claudius, Emperor, 7, 23, 34, 53,
  57, 77, 79, 93–6, 116–9.
  his building policy, 93–6, 119.
  role in Fucine Lake project, 93,
  95.
  role in Harbor of Ostia, 77, 79.
  relationship with factotums,
  116–9.
  role in aqueduct building, 93, 95.
Cleopatra, 3.
client, 108.
Cohortes Vigilium, 25, 43.
Columella, 117.
Concord, temple of, 23.
conductores (see contractors)
contractors, 34–5, 59, 72, 88, 95.
congiaria, 53.
Corinth, 4, 97.
  canal, 97.
Cornelius Sabinus, 114.

cuniculi, 61, 67.
curatores, 33, 106.

Davies, O., 64–5.
Dio, 7, 53, 77, 81, 85, 98, 111, 114.
Diribitorium, 25, 43.
dole, 36.
domus, 131.
  calculation of WUs, 131.
Domus Aurea, 25–6, 97, 131.
Domus Tiberiana, 25, 51.
Domus Transitoria, 25–6.
Duff, 117.
Duncan-Jones, R., 20, 57.

eat, drink and be merry, 5–6, 119.
Egypt, 3, 79–80, 104.
  grain supply, 79.
emergency clean-up, 38, 69.
Emperor
  as executive branch ix.
Empire
  economic conditions, 11, 38,
  103–4.
epitomator, of Aurelius Victor,
  100.
Etruria, 79.
exodus from Rome, 37.
expropriation of mines, 49.

factotum, xi, 107–20.
  definition of, 107.
  of Augustus, 109–12.
  of Tiberius, 112–3.
  of Caligula, 113–6.
  of Claudius, 116–9.
  of Nero, 119–20.
  difference vs. client and patron,
  108.
  use of freedmen as, 116–9.
familia Caesaris, 34.
famine, in Rome, 5, 47, 77.
financial crisis of A.D. 33, 10, 38,
  48–9.
fires, 38, 96–8.
  fire of A.D. 64, 96, 98.
Flavians, 118.
Fletcher, Bannister, 21.
fiscus, 47–8, 50.

food supply, i, 5, 47, 53, 77, 79–
80.
Forbes, R., 64–5, 83.
Forum of Augustus, 25, 43; **110**.
Frank, Tenney, 12, 38, 48–9, 57,
117.
freedmen, as factotums, 116–20.
Frontinus, 18, 113.
Fucine Lake, x, 10, 15, 20, 47, 53,
57–76; **58**.
as outlier project, x.
general project, 61.
features and size, 59.
variation in depth, 59.
archaeological details, 61–3; **60**.
shift work, 65–7.
work crew output, 63–4; **62**.
bricklayers, 67–8.
accidents and emergencies,
68–9.
calculation data, Appendix 3,
141–4.
indirect labor, 70.
seasonal use of aqueduct labor,
72.
depth of, 59.
nature and size of task, 61–2.
size of crew, 63.
comparison to mining, 64–5.
direct labor needs, 67–8.
minimum completion time, 68.
water problems, 69.
epidemics, 69.
slips, cave-ins and tunnel
collapses, 69.
dimensions of tunnel, 61.
shafts, 61, 63.
workdays, 68.
comparison with modern labor,
70.
alternate explanation for labor
numbers, 71.
proximity to aqueducts, 72.
transfer of labor between
projects, 72, 95.

Gaius, Emperor, see Caligula
Gaul, 4.
Glotz, 66.
Goodchild, R.G., 83.

Gracchus, Tiberius, 79.
Growth of empire, 3–4.
Gymnasium of Nero, 96.

Hadrian, Emperor, 59.
Harbor of Ostia, see Ostia
Herkert, C.H., 97.
Hopkins, Keith, 39, 50.
Hopper, R.J., 64, 66.
House of Vestals, 25–6.

identification of projects, 15–9.
selection, 15.
identification of projects, see
Appendix 2, 135–9.
Illyricum, 4.
Imperial civil servants, 34.
indexing approach to
quantification, 19–20.
individual project evaluation, 19.
inflation, 51, 97.
innovation, 11, 38, 105, 107.
insulae, 10–1.
irregular manpower demand, 36–9.

Jones, A.H.M., 34.
Josephus, 5, 99.
Julia, daughter of Augustus, 109.
Julio-Claudian
earlier, 41–55.
later, 93–101.
Julius, see Caesar
Juglar cycle, 26.
Juvenal, 22.

Keynes, J.M., 11, 104.
Kondratieff cycle, 26.

labor management, 31–9.
labor supply, 34.
demand for, 34.
free labor, disadvantages, 35.
slave versus free labor, x, 34–5,
37.
sources of, 34, 36.
labor management, 34–6.
Laurion, mine, 66.
Leonardo da Vinci airport, 81.
Levick, Barbara, 49, 53, 111.
limitation of study, 10, 15.

Linares, 66.
Liris, river, 61.
literary sources, 6–7, 10, 115–6.

Macro, praetorian prefect, 113–4.
macro-economics, 26, 103–5.
macro-boom, 41.
Maecenas, 109, 111.
Magna Mater, temple of, 21–2.
Maison Carrée, work unit base,
    20–1, 23; **cover, 17.**
Management systems, 34, 104–7.
man-day, 19.
Manpower costs, 15–24.
    determination of, see Appendix
    1, 131–4.
manubiae, 32, 106.
Mare Nostrum, 79.
Marsi, 59, 73.
Marius, 111.
Martial, 100.
Mausoleum of Augustus, **45.**
Meiggs, R., 47, 61, 85.
Metellus, L., 33.
Middleton, 22.
Millar, Fergus, 117.
mini-boom, 41.
Momigliano, A., 99.
mos maiorum, 41, 106–7, 115, 121.
Mount Salviano, **60.**
multiplier, 103–4.

Naples, 79.
Narcissus, imperial freedman, 71,
    96, 108, 116, 118.
Nero, Emperor, 7, 11, 87, 119–20;
    86.
    civil unrest, 96.
    his building program, 96–7.
    biases against him, 97–8.
    relationships with factotums,
        119–20.
    fire of A.D. 64, 96–7.
    attitude of Christian Church, 98.
    financial troubles, 97.
    pro-Neronian tradition, 99–100.
    his quinquennium, 99, 119.
    his harbor project, 96.
    his Thermae project, 96.
Neronian Nemesis, 97–100.

Neronian Nirvana, 96–7.
Nîmes, 20–1.
novus homo, 111.
Numidia, 79.

objectives of study, 6–7, 10–2.
Octavian, see Augustus
Octavius, Gaius, 32.
Oost, 118.
organization of book, ix–x.
Ostia, harbor of, x, 10, 37, 47, 53,
    57, 77–91; **78, 82, 86, 91, 146.**
    as key port, 77–8.
    as outlier project, x.
    planning for the harbor, 5.
    Augustus' plan, 5.
    take charge of grain supply, 5.
    reasons for inclusion, 10.
    project description, 81.
    nature of the harbor, 80.
    analysis of plan, 81–8.
    manpower conclusions, 88–90.
    mole-building, 84–5.
    land-based work vs. water-borne
        work, 84–5, 88.
    completion dating, 87–8.
    seasonal use of labor, 89.
    calculations on, Appendix 4,
        145–9.
    location, 80.
    nature of area, 80.
    alternate approaches to
        construction, 81–3.
    dimensions, 83.
    construction details, 80–3.
    diagram of, 78.
    digging methods, 84–5.
    calculation of manpower needs—
        ox, man, Appendix 4, 145–9.
    evaluation of manpower costs,
        Appendix 4, 145–9.
    source of labor, 88–9.
    timing, 87–8.
    seasonality of shipping, 89.
    possibility of completion by
        Nero, 87–8.
    as a food port, 79.
    recent airport excavations, 81.
    loss of 200 ships, 87.

Nero's coin, 86–7; **86**.
choice of digging methods, 83–4.
transfer of labor between
projects, 88–9.
Otho, emperor, 99.

Packer, J.E., 11.
Pallas, imperial freedman, 96, 108,
118.
Pax Romana, 3.
Pergamum, 4.
Petronius, author, 39.
physical needs of empire, 3, 5–6.
Pigors, Paul, 108, 116.
plagues, 38.
Platner-Ashby, 18–9.
Pliny the Elder, 49, 66, 97, 117.
Plutarch, 79.
Po valley, 79.
political stability, 4.
Pompey, the general, 106.
Pompey, theater of, 23, 25.
Pomptine marshes, 47, 77, 79.
Poppaea, Sabina, 96.
Porta Praenestina, **54**.
porticoes, 131.
    calculation of WUs, 131.
Praetorian Guard, 113, 119–20.
private building, 18–9, 38–9, 103.
project by project measurement,
    x–xi.
propaganda, 6, 24, 32.
project identification, x, 15–9.
Province of Asia, 4.
psychological needs, 3–6.
public works administration, see
    labor management
Puteoli, harbor of, 79.

quinquennium, Nero's, 100, 119.
Quintilian, 77.

Reinhold, Meyer, 111.
Res Gestae, 7, 18, 24, 32, 41, 44.
restoration of the aqueducts, 5–6,
    44.
Rickman, Geoffrey, 89.
Rodewald, Cosmo, 48–49.

Rome, passim.
food supply, 5.
transportation system, 79.
Roman Revolution, ix, 4.

Saepta Julia, 22–4, 43.
Salviano, Mount, 61; **60**.
Sardinia, 79.
Satyricon, 39.
Schumpeter, Joseph, 11, 38.
Sejanus, praetorian prefect, 108–9,
    112–3.
Senate, Roman, ix, 31–3, 106.
    furnishing finance, 31.
    losing control of building
        program, 33.
    part of deliberative branch, ix.
Seneca, the Younger, 11, 77, 96,
    100, 108, 119–20.
    study of apartment housing, 11.
Sicily, 79.
Sippel, Donald V., 36, 84, 89.
slaves, 34–5.
    relationship with freemen, 35.
    use of, 34.
    sources for, 34, 118–9.
    owner's attitude towards, 34–6.
    protection for, 34–6.
Spain, 4, 66.
    gold mining, 66.
Statue of Claudia, 22.
Strabo, 11.
Strong, D.E., 32–3, 105–6.
Suetonius, 7, 49, 53, 57, 61, 71, 81,
    98–9, 113–6.
Sulla, the dictator, his public
    works program, 32–33, 106.
Syme, Ronald, ix, x, 7, 120.

Tacitus, 7, 53, 87, 96, 98, 112, 115,
    118.
Temple of Capitoline Jupiter, 32.
Temple of Concord, 23.
Temple of Magna Mater, 22–3.
Temple of Rome and Augustus, 10.
Terracina, 77.
Testaguzza, Otello, 81, 83.
theater, 132.
    calculation of WUs, see
        Appendix 1, 131–4.

Theater of Balbus, 25, 26, 41, 43,
    46.
Theater of Marcellus, 25, 26, 41,
    43, 46; **42**.
Theater of Pompey, 25.
Thermae Agrippae, 26, 41; **8, 9**.
Thermae Neronianae, 25, 26.
Third Punic War, 3.
Tiber, river, 79–80.
Tiberian Trough, 46–51.
Tiberius, xii, 5, 7, 23, 46–53,
    112–3.
    as factotum, 111
    and Agrippa's death, 46.
    dearth of tasks, 46–7.
    food crises, 5, 47.
    lack of money, 47.
    privy purse, 47.
    financial analysis, 47–50.
    financial crisis, 49.
    commitment to penury, 49.
    destruction rate for small coins,
        50.
    as corn mover, 5, 47.
    unable to resolve famine, 5, 47.
    his building policy, 46–7, 112.
    his monetary policy, 47–50.
    relationship to factotums, 112–3.

Tigellinus, praetorian prefect, 120.
time limits of study, 15.
Tivoli, 113.

Torlonia, Prince, 59.
Trajan, Emperor, 59.
    his remark on Nero, 99–100.
Treggiari, Susan, 118.
tunneling, 44, 61, 63, 95.

underemployment, see
    unemployment
unemployed, 37, 51.
unemployment, 36, 38–9, 51.
urban violence, 6, 96.

Van Deman, 18.
Vercingetorix, 4.
vertical integration, 70.
Vespasian, Emperor, 98.
Victor, Aurelius, 99.
    his epitomator, 100.
Vipsanius family, see Agrippa
Vitellius, Emperor, 99.

Water Board, 33.
water supply, 5, 41.
Westermann, W.L., 35.
White, K.D., 89.
Wiseman, T.P., 111.
Work Units (WU), definition of use
    in study, 20–2.
WU, see Work Units

Yavetz, Z., 53, 96.